A SAFE PLACE

Also by Leston Havens:

MAKING CONTACT
APPROACHES TO THE MIND

A Safe Place

Leston Havens

BALLANTINE BOOKS • NEW YORK

All rights reserved under International and Pan-American Copyright Conventions. Published in the United States by Ballantine Books, a division of Random House, Inc., New York, and distributed in Canada by Random House of Canada Limited, Toronto.

"The Writer" from *The Mind Reader*, copyright © 1971 by Richard Wilbur, reprinted by permission of Harcourt Brace Jovanovich, Inc., and Faber and Faber, Ltd.

Library of Congress Catalog Card Number: 90-93225

ISBN: 0-345-37060-0

This edition published by arrangement with Harvard University Press, Cambridge.

Cover design by James R. Harris
Cover illustration by Charles Bjorklund

Manufactured in the United States of America
First Ballantine Books Edition: February 1991
10 9 8 7 6 5 4 3 2 1

For Emily
and her great-grandmother,
Emily Edith Marie

PREFACE

The work of psychological healing begins in a safe place, to be compared with the best of hospital experience or, from an earlier time, church sanctuary. The psychological safe place permits the individual to make spontaneous, forceful gestures and, at the same time, represents a community that both allows the gestures and is valued for its own sake. It stands at the crossroads of society and solitude, at the intersection of those often divergent and equally necessary paths leading to ourselves and to what we need for ourselves—others. In this safe place, created by doctor and patient, we can learn our inhibitions, false alliances, community-denying demands, and why we despair of anything better; and, still more important, experience these bits of sickness within a deft association that provides tolerance and hope. Finally, this little community serves as a preliminary, general model for those eventual, particular lives we search for outside it.

A psychotherapy and psychiatry devoted both to self-assertion and to society embraces, by that one intention, the various emphases given the work by each of the great schools. But how, in actual day-to-day fact, does one establish a person or measure the force of society and others? And how is the unstable equilibrium of self-assertion and the demands of society to be maintained within the microcosm of psychotherapy? How, in other words, do we set about making a safe psychological place?

In this book I extend my earlier studies on the specifics of psychological intervention originating from the various schools of psychiatry and psychology. The emergence of psychotherapeutics has often been serendipitous. Each school tends to generalize its contribution as appropriate for every clinical situation, whether that contribution is disease diagnosis, existential empathy, psychoanalytic free association, behavioral conditioning, or the managerial attitudes and devices of social psychiatry. Only over time do specific indications emerge for the use of each discovery. (The same has been true of such physical interventions as phenothiazines or electric shock therapy.) Throughout the book I try to show how the major contributions of the schools may be selected to form more flexible and effective tools of therapy. I make bold in Chapter 2, for example, to point out what I think are the indications for classical psychoanalysis narrowly defined. In the following chapter I go on to discuss the most recently introduced of all these methods, performative statements, which offers a fresh approach to some of the most difficult problems in psychotherapy.

I write for the general reader, as much as for the professional, and therefore set the specifics of intervention into a background of broad psychiatric information and the dilemmas confronted by practitioners. Beginning with a relatively simple instance of safe-place making, I move to successively more difficult cases. In Chapters 4 and 5, I reconceive the interview, first around a particularly elusive case and then more systematically, around the specific drawbacks of too tight an application of preconceived theories. Chapters 6, 7, and 8 address the unsafest of cases, suicidal, psychotic, and psychopathic, and some of the means by which a degree of safety can be introduced. I close speculatively, asking what the extraordinary Harry Stack Sullivan might tell us if he were alive and why the future belongs, as I believe it does, to this work.

In the interest of readability, I have omitted references from the text; a section at the end includes relevant scholarly material. The human beings referred to have been disguised by changes in such major characteristics as nationality or gender and also in some details that are the most revealing signatures of all. With the inevitable loss of scientific rigor that such a protection of personal rights entails, these cases are best seen as illustrations or hypothetical types. It is the details of my treatments, and the speculations about what treatment can be, that are the book's heart.

CONTENTS

Making a
Safe Place

CHAPTER 1

MY DOCTOR

The patient sat down promptly, decisively, as if my office were the right place to be. I was not all that sure. For this man in his late fifties did not appear decisive by temperament, perhaps more wise: he was rumpled, the bell of a stethoscope peeking out of one pocket, overweight, at once cheerful and depressed, a little tired and diffident. Maybe his sure sitting down was a relieved settling in.

He smiled at me and I sensed immediately why he was such a successful doctor. I was warmed by the smile and at the same time surveyed by an experienced eye. Further, he spoke right up. If I had any impulse to question him, it was preempted by his detailed, open, sequential review of symptoms and events—capped by a diagnosis, in fact several, an impressive psychological formulation, and they by the opinions of my predecessor therapists, all learned, well known, and, in his presence at least, clever and clear.

This was my first glimpse of him. I had two reactions. In the presence of so much industry and intelligence, could I be clever and clear? In the light of that industry and intelligence, should

I do anything at all? Perhaps I should simply admire. If he rivaled me, or left me helpless, I was under no obligation either to compete or to fix what worked so well.

Then he said he was afraid he would die. He struck an almost musing note, as if not to alarm me. Did he know this therapeutic work so well that he also knew its first requirement: the two parties should not frighten each other away? Quietly he told me he had suffered one heart attack, expected another, and was being treated by several specialists. Meantime he watched his body like an unpredictable enemy, an enemy all around, at his very heart.

In the silence that followed, I felt the mercilessness of the body, which secures its sovereignty of our happiness by an unrivaled intimacy: we can never leave it, except in death and imagination; we are abjectly dependent on it for our greatest delights; it is the messenger of pain, even shapes our identity. There is no evidence, surely, of a sick mind in being uneasy about the company of a sick body. If the first requirement of psychological work is to create a safe place, a little hospital in which patients can show any sickness and reach any health, how could I bring this man safety with such an enemy at his heart?

Once he had been hospitalized, sedated, freed from pain, investigated, and treated. It was a very busy, complicated place, so vulnerable is the body, so subtle its workings. I knew that many of the conditions for a safe mental place resemble those for the body. There are psychological contagions as invasive as viruses; there may be events inviting disapproval and remonstrance; psychological pain, whether in the form of anxiety, sadness, rage, or yearning, calls out for analgesics like an open wound. Psychological observing also teaches the same lesson as student microscopy: don't put your finger on the slide. But what is the state of the art? Can we keep fingers off the slide?

Meanwhile he looked at me in his sympathetic, curious way,

and I looked back, not, I hope, too differently. I had another hope: that he would not die. I don't mean that I already cared about him in the way I care about some others. Perhaps I only hoped he would not die right here, in my office, under my care. We both knew how troublesome that can be. No, I was not pretending to any great, loving friendship. Psychotherapy is full of these ironies and ambiguities. Sympathetic as we felt, for example, neither would expect to be here long if he didn't pay, which is another reason to hope he would live. So I said, "I hope you're wrong." I almost added, "Not to imply that life is worth living." Many despairing people need to hear that, but it would have seemed odd with this successful man.

Such is what I mean by the state of the art, the means available. The patient was certainly cooperative. More than that, he offered himself up. It became easy to imagine why his patients failed to pay, as he told me, or overstayed their times. He might exhaust himself in this giving, either with his patients or as mine.

The story he told was at once moving and familiar, with that element of singularity clinging to every human story. The patient had been born abroad, in a beleagured country from which his parents made desperate efforts to escape. The father went ahead to America, leaving his family behind, at an age when the boy could proudly take his place and at the same time yearn for him. Whether because she was an ambitious and possessive woman or because the nature of the lively boy and these circumstances conspired to bring such qualities out, the mother fostered the boy's eagerness to succeed in the father's absence and later even in his presence when the father himself was not so successful, making this a project with all the steadiness of purpose and opportunities for criticism of any well-managed enterprise. The boy therefore entered the safer life of this country—after they had finally arrived—with a settled and exciting goal, an organizing idea that was both his own and not his own. He would please his mother, he would all at once imitate, rival, and replace his father, and do so with a wonderfully enthusiastic and convincing feeling that the whole enterprise was his.

I felt this theme of service in the very telling of the tale. I who was now his servant was being served. He did not whine, cavil, or correct: he served it all up. My temptation—to remind him that his story was only one of a great number that could be told about his life—was resisted, out of sheer gratitude. A contentious patient might have provoked more effort on my part. This was unfortunate because the reminder might serve our enterprise, to open up other possibilities of both meaning and life.

So here was the first danger to his safety with me, a danger springing from his many admirable qualities. The orderliness, cooperativeness, the sharp intelligence of his account, all threatened him with a fresh imprisonment. I felt my mind close down around the "formulation," windows of doubt shutting one by one. Again I wondered if there was anything for me to do.

Of course I could "explain" what he had said, serving it back with a different garnish. The familiar story of parental ambitions merging with an eager child's need for a life, for example, offered the possibility of being pushed beyond one's limits, like a swimmer in a desperate current. Perhaps this was the half-conscious content of his fear of dying. But what would it be like to hear one's life summed up so neatly, even to the inclusion of the final, terrifying symptom? The implication was, "You are drowning, perhaps have always been drowning."

Beware, I thought, of surgeons who thirst to operate. Away with medicines, they say, with physiotherapy, even heat and cold: give me that knife. Many psychotherapists are no different. Hearing a well-told tale or ingeniously recoding a poorly told one, they thirst to explain. Psychological explanations abound. We have interpreted the ancient mysteries of man- and woman-kind: dreams, madness, love itself. Give most of us a microphone or a sheet of paper or a receptive patient, or best of all a depressed patient expecting to hear the worst, and nothing is beyond us. This is one reason Freud has been so important: he poured out explanations.

But Freud, the greatest of explainers, was also one of the wisest. All cases, he warned, suffer from being explained. The best treatment results spring on therapists who are willing to be surprised, therapists who put off formulations until the work is done. The "evenly suspended attention" he recommended as the ideal therapeutic attitude meant no concentration on particulars, no predicting or review. Moreover, the meaning of anything heard now cannot be understood until much later, often when the case is closed.

So I expressed my hope. I believe I continued to look sympathetic, and a bit aloof, as if to convey that all the returns weren't in. This is a characteristic posture of mine; it can appear condescending, perhaps is. But I hoped in this case to convey just enough uncertainty to leave his mind open and not so much that he would be driven to fresh efforts of service.

But perhaps this was what led him to change his theme. He said he had recently seen a girl—she could not have been more than seventeen or eighteen—at the local supermarket. He had found himself following her; they had had some sort of shopping-cart collision and then again in another aisle. It was all quite ludicrous, and yet there was no puzzlement or laughter in his eye. He said the first collision had occurred in the fruit department and he loved fruit.

If he had not been, if only momentarily, so solemn, I might have burst out laughing. But the solemnity had a sadness about it, and the collision very much the quality of an accident: they had turned a corner coming from opposite directions and he had to get down on all fours to rescue her little juice cans. I was too taken up in the details even to smile. Afterward, he said, he felt this was the story of his life, bumping into things, America, his mother, medicine, his wife, his heart, and him on all fours, accidents not service.

It was a happy accident for me. I am a firm believer in chance, I have had my shopping-cart collisions, I worry about my heart, I even like fruit. We were together. One little juice can he had not retrieved, however; he went away feeling he had failed the attractive young woman. Discarding his solemnity, he remarked how silly it all was.

All through his marriage he had felt responsible for his wife's happiness, he abruptly said. It was not so much that he wanted to please her as he was afraid he would not. This, I suspected, was his first real confession; he seemed ashamed to say it to me. He may have thought I was fearless before women and that he had violated the male code. Could I like him if he felt so subservient? Perhaps he was right. Did I now feel superior, as a proper doctor might, to my suffering patient down on all fours, fearful of women, perhaps seeking me out in order to become a real man?

It was certainly time to dispel that notion, or else the safety of my place would be threatened anew. Any macho expectations would deny this frightened, tired man not only freedom but rest, which I more and more was thinking he needed. So I said, "Well, she may not be capable of gratitude," leaving the *she* as just that, to be any woman who came to mind. At first he looked puzzled, then grateful, and proceeded, with gathering momentum, to voice his resentments. Probably I had opened a door to those resentments, by not increasing the possible expectations of either male responsibility or fearlessness, and by directing a not altogether friendly attention back to the wife.

Indeed his movement was now straight and rapid. Many, many things he had done to please her, but she became grouchier and grouchier. This man liked to please people—I had seen that—and he was failing lamentably with her. The more she complained, the more he felt to blame. She raised the rewards higher and higher, and he jumped more and more frantically. There was a curious little thing he liked her to do in making love; it was one of those strikingly particular signatures of desire, a gesture, just a turn of the head. Once she had done it with seeming delight. Now it was a distant prize so attractive he could sometimes think of nothing else. Worst of all, he became ashamed to ask for it.

There had developed a gross imbalance of power, which reminded him of the relationship with his mother. He felt that his demands were shameful; she seemed to have no scruples about hers. He therefore presented himself to me as someone excessively demanding, guilty, and ready for the most painful psychopathological scrutiny. This he had received. If a doctor, like a plumber or electrician, can find nothing wrong, he has nothing to do. In this case, there had seemed much to do. For starters, he was masochistic and narcissistic, he said.

I remarked to myself that the treatment had become like his homelife, a distressing opportunity for accusations and guilt between unequal parties. Maybe he had persuaded his earlier helpers that he was indeed the flawed creature he felt. Certainly any therapist eager to fix a flaw had only to ask him. The reader must know such reactions too. What student of psychiatric descriptions has not felt himself or herself in every one? Because we all have so much in common and no means of quantitation, it is nothing to see the same monstrosities everywhere, in patients, therapists, readers themselves.

I sensed an even greater danger. As long as therapists depend upon patients' accounts of their problems, we are in danger of seeing things the way the patients do. This may be "empathic," but it can also be wrong-headed and demoralizing. Psychological reporting discloses a paradox that reverses negative and positive, figure and ground. Modest people, because of their modesty, often describe themselves as pretentious or, worse, megalomanic. On the other hand, genuinely megalomanic people see themselves as modest, as concealing or underplaying their great gifts. Take my patient's conviction that he was demanding. Really demanding people, in my experience, seldom view themselves as demanding; they feel entitled to even more than they receive. In my interaction with this man I noted that he was extravagantly giving. If he wanted something back for all this largesse, it would hardly be surprising, especially in view of my job. Yet here too he put very modest demands on my performance.

I remembered a moment in my own childhood when I had felt unexpectedly and painfully rejected and then to blame. I was sitting up in bed with measles; my mother told me my father was leaving the family. She felt very much to blame herself, so much so that she could hardly recognize, much less dispel, my small sense of responsibility, or what may have been its underside, my wish; she did not contradict me. Nor would it have been effective now to contradict my patient's insistence. That lay much further ahead. At this point the patient felt his responsibility everywhere, for his wife's happiness, his patients', the success of this treatment, the soundness of his heart. Such was the first glimpse I had of his singularity, this taking of responsibility. It was a kind of adventurousness, carried up onto the plain of duty, steadiness, and caring.

No doubt the reader has her or his matching memories, which spring up like spirits to give personal meaning to any impinging human event. It is this meaning-making that brings psychological work its special joys and dangers. Could I listen to my patient objectively, as one might observe an inanimate object, when I had just joined his sorrow to perhaps the most poignant moment of my life?

I could sigh, and probably did. The reader looking down at this page may have sighed too. But you could just as well have thrown the book aside with contempt for such soft sentiments and subjectivity. Get me a real doctor, you might have said. Let us analyze, medicate, even operate. At least present a hard-nosed reason for all these sighs and sympathies.

Safety, I would reply, safety. Should anyone operate without safe conditions? Believe it or not, this is what I was trying to provide. It was in the interest of safety that I followed my sigh with words I hoped would surprise him. Later I learned that he expected me to reprimand him for his self-blaming (adding this blame to his own), to point out the dead-ended, masochistic coloring of all this responsibility. He was wallowing, he expected me to say, in his grand sense of importance, suffering in his superior dutifulness, a plump, aging, self-conscious Christ on the cross.

Instead I remarked, half to myself, on the dangers of modesty and responsibility. I may have trotted out that old saying: no good deed goes unpunished. I wanted to shake gently the assumptions he presented: that he was immodest, irresponsible, wholly to blame. I did not expect or even want him to "get it," in the sense of grasping exactly what I meant and where it could lead him. That would have been to substitute an act of thought, which might have been no more than a rationalization, for the start of a deep sea change of attitudes and beliefs. Moreover, an elucidation would have set my ideas against his, really my authority against his, which might be a dangerous situation indeed. Worst of all, to contradict him at this point, and in open discussion that could hardly be avoided, would be to shame him on a moral level, telling him he was wrong and should have been thinking a different way.

I don't want to bully the reader either. But because you sit outside and above this exercise, a desperate note readily permeates any effort to enlist and convince you. One runs up flags, invokes authorities, does everything but rise off the page and grab the other's throat. An old teacher of mine liked to say, "If you have to tell someone something, it's already too late." These repentant sentences, as well, may seem tardy and conniving. It is the same way I felt with my patient: there was much I would like to do, but the instruments at hand, oh those instruments!

There we were, two people, sitting together, one feeling in great danger, the other almost equally concerned with danger, both seeking safety. It was not immediately apparent that we were in fact at the sharpest possible cross-purposes, and for a reason that seemed to grow and spread the more one contemplated it. The simple fact was that the only safety my patient could imagine was in being sick. The heart attack had for a while moderated his wife's discontent, just as his mother had treated him best when he was ill. Moreover, his whole professional life was given over to sickness; then he too was gentlest and most caring. Safety was in sickness, even if it meant living at the edge of death. I thought to myself that he put his physical symptoms before him like talismans to ward off evil spirits.

What narrative drama the present story has is in undoing this bodily drama, which is also the psychotherapeutic drama: safety established apart from sickness. The narrator, who was also the therapist, stands between the patient and the reader like an anxious host, fearing stagnation, wondering what is in each of their minds, not so much enlightening the scene as finding parts of his own mind that act upon the scene, and most often by hopeful inaction. As Robert Frost said of the working poet, he is waiting for something to occur to him, something in the case of both poem and psychotherapy that is moving.

Of course the movement I wanted here was away from sickness, little as I knew what health meant for this particular man. At first I wondered if it meant leaving his wife; certainly I hoped to balance her sometimes devastating power. But what occurred to me proved to be in fact usually nothing at all, that at most I should just be there, an inaction that may baffle the reader far more than it did the patient.

Sometimes I consoled myself in my passivity with Napoleon's supreme desiderata of generalship, inexhaustible patience and utter decisiveness. It is the apparent absence of the latter that may explain the different responses of my doctor and my reader. I was told long ago by a respected teacher that therapists should not say whatever they feel they must say: interventions should be free. I added to that a rule of my own: say nothing when nothing occurs to me to say. This too is a kind of freedom. My patient may have tolerated my silence because it gave him freedom: I may have passed my freedom on to him. But the reader has bought this book for an end different from my doctor's purchase of treatment. It is the difference between an observer and a participant. The first would like to hear something; the second wants to make his own speech.

My patient certainly did that. The story he now told was as different from his theory of accidents as that had been from the story of service. He might have been a different man. I have often noted that the consistency, regularity, almost homogeneity we think we see in people is a product of our need to have one person before us, a whole, habitual creature, when in fact so-called multiple personalities are really only the sharply etched version of what occurs in everyone. This is part of the appeal of novels and plays. The author makes up characters to represent something, giving us the solid but really misleading conviction that we understand someone. Eventually my patient taught me what I had learned many times before, that we are all at bottom very much alike—just as the surgeon opening up any of us finds approximately the same heart, lungs, and viscera—but that the likeness puts on many changing configurations, one moment dominated by rage or pretending, another moment by a myste-rious sullenness or a mysterious joy. Personality is not nearly so distinct as you would conclude from books, which may be why the books all disagree. What the patient now revealed—and this was over several months—illustrates human variety, even cha-meleonship.

The man I see now, he told me, is not the man he once was. He had left home on a motorcycle, raced across the continent like an inebriated eagle. (Where was my plump Christ then?) One weekend in Nevada he invaded a jazz ensemble and played all night. But he was not drunk, not even high; he felt free, sure, full of himself and adventure. This was also the spirit in which he went to medical school. Even after a year and a half of reading, memorizing, straight donkey work, it still felt like a lark. As he spoke he sounded as if he had been shot out of a gun.

Nor was this all the high spirits of youth. For thirty years he had been the moving force of several theatrical groups, as actor, director, once author. He told me he had often imagined giving up doctoring altogether, to ride the slippery theater rails forever, to play and dream but also to be what he liked to be as a doctor too, the technician, student, sometime trickster. He set me to thinking, is he really a doctor or an impostor, one of those genius impostors better at our professions than the profession-als? But I could as well have wondered the other way around: is he really an actor, or only imagining himself one?

His variety comforted me, and I did not think he was an impostor. Impostors have to be impostors; he could play at be-ing one. He had access to a great part of his humanity; little of him seemed walled off. Surely health is defined by this range, the way the bone-and-joint doctors measure the range of motion in a limb. And the conventionality he possessed was carried lightly, not armor but a mask. You could catch him now and then smiling behind it. I also had many occasions to see him correcting and balancing himself. Extravagant thoughts were entertained and then brought down to earth. Thank God, I thought, and wise is my silence, my talk unnecessary.

It also occurred to me that this sickness, at least his kind of preoccupation with sickness, was partly the form humans give to their need for safety—so we might not be at such cross-purposes. Poverty does not give safety, or madness or passivity, as a rule. But the presentation of sickness is like the wolf's upturned throat; it usually ends warfare and elicits kindness and help. He might be doing this until he could mobilize other resources. I began to wonder if our senses of safety were not extending in parallel lines. I was more and more comfortable with him, and had growing confidence. He also expressed growing confidence in me, though it reassured me much more that he quite visibly relaxed and spoke more freely; color came into his face. Don't only listen to patients, I tell students. Watch them, watch their bodies—which cannot lie.

My little hospital, I though complacently, was operating well. The various tissues were coming into view, and they seemed healthy, even robust. Moreover, I felt I could really see them; the patient appeared more and more real. It was not like those cases where one searches and does not find, or, still more different, where one rides broncos of feeling, making each interview a rodeo of suspense. A great, steady range of affects, and that cousin of affects, humor, paraded before me: sadness, yearning, anxiety, and the characteristic bittersweet reaction to romantic disillusionment, even occasional rage, though here he was restricted. His humor showed itself in many ways. He was a wonderful storyteller, and then the note of self-depreciation in his character turned into fun. Humor depends upon maintaining simultaneous perspectives and rapidly changing emotions. He was capable of both and loved the closely related play of paradox. All this is to say that he dwelt easily with much of himself, and at the center was a self capable of shifting views, self-correction, self-mockery.

Any reader seeing my enjoyment of this splendid man might be tempted to join the chorus of those critics of psychotherapy who term it paid friendship—and it was true that he didn't have friends in the sense of others with whom he was both open and close. If friendship were not so often paid for in ways far more costly than psychotherapy—as when friends turn out to be predatory enemies—those critics could not be silenced. But as soon as one demands of friendship mutual respect and some happy resonance of interests and styles, there should be no surprise at its rarity or the occasional good sense of paying for it. Of course I say this here defensively, but not in defense against my patient, who had suffered many pains of intimacy. And, I thought, how we pay! It is not a question of nothing for nothing, but of paying heavily for very little. Self-directed death wishes, masochistic instincts, poor selections, the idealization of suffering, a compliance that brings out the worst in others—there are possibilities enough. But what to do about it? Again, the instruments, the instruments!

His pains seemed to come and go with the rising and falling demands of both his wife and his patients, with whom he was often on closer terms, in the sense of emotional rapport, than he was with his wife. Part of that pain was as natural as the stiffness and fatigue that follow muscular exercise. This is a hard point to make because of the widespread yearning to pin some pathological onus on patients, to discover a villain, a psychological cancer, whenever human life departs from the ideal of universal safety and comfort. My patient would have been the first to deride that expectation; body, mind, society are hardly designed so well. But with his adventurous sense of responsibility he was ready to take it all on himself.

Safety I had put first, and inside that safe place a number of stories appeared, each inviting a brief epiphany of reach and grasp. With each story came more and more of him, this man who was so largely healthy and effective. But for all his growing confidence in me and presence in the room, the pain continued, his fear of death, his sacrifice and responsibility. Was it merely that he was not yet safe enough, was he too tired and over-worked, was he in love with pain? Each group of interviews served up another epiphany of conclusion around which we could rally. I resisted.

So now it was my resistance to concluding and not his, as is traditionally the case, because I did not see how concluding could improve him, even if there were a way to know which account of his life was finally the true one. My faith was in the process. But I could as well write that my faith was in Allah for all the word *process* might mean to either patient or reader. Once the patient asked me, what was I doing? This is seldom an easy moment. One does not want to turn therapy into a course on therapy. Though he seemed entitled to know, perhaps especially as a fellow doctor, again I resisted. Nor was I eager to say, trust me. That would sound like trust in Allah, when it was himself I hoped he could trust.

And yet I welcomed the embarrassing question. It was a sig-nal of felt equality, comradeship, intelligent curiosity, maybe a giving up of blind faith. I was tempted to say, "I wish I knew"— which I have said when I felt the other's faith and confidence in me were of psychotic proportions. But, again, this man was not like that.

Luckily, the mystery of the process cleared somewhat not long after. I don't recall that I had ever used the word *safety* with him, so I was pleased to hear him say he felt safer here than he ever remembered feeling, and then still later that in this safe place he experimented with being himself. It reminded me of what D. W. Winnicott recommended to mothers, that they let the child be alone with them, that they not intrude on the child's emerging selfhood. It reminded me too of the fundamental rule of psychoanalysis—to free-associate, to say whatever comes to mind—which may be the first time the word *freedom* enters medicine. A safe place where he would be free, recovering in this protected freedom what he might have lost, or creating something new.

I don't think he knew how much of my energy went into making the place safe. Perhaps that's why his appreciation of safety sounded so good to my ears. It helped me resist saying, "You haven't always made it easy, you who so invite criticism, diagnosis, deep and penetrating interpretations, confirmations of your guilt and responsibility." The greatest power of psychotherapy may be precisely this power not to confirm the patients' expectations, not to collude in the games they and their personal world have long played, but, slowly, to turn them toward a more natural and happy course.

CHAPTER 2

FREUD'S INVENTION

Freud invented, in the silences of psychoanalysis, a method of correcting a particular human problem so specific and effective as to defy any substitution or even alteration. A great invention is like a piece of great wit: it seems in retrospect the only answer. Recall G. K. Chesterton's reply to the question, What book would you most like with you on a desert island? "Huntington's Guide to Practical Shipbuilding." Freud's invention is like that.

Imagine a young person very attractive and a little uncertain. Imagine further a mother of this only child a little hovering, a little too eager to be helpful and advisory. This not uncommon situation puts the young person at risk of what we can term "imagined incapacity": the half-conviction of being unable to do all sorts of things that in fact she probably can do. Of course the imagined incapacity has to be explained, justified to its possessor, and to this end the various bodily sensations and mental preoccupations that everyone has, of anxiety and uncertainty, signals that any close listener to the body's vicissitudes will be able to hear—these "explain" the hesitancy. The sensations and preoccupations provide reasons for worry and doubt that no student of life and the body need be without.

Beneath this little drama of hesitation lies another. Freud also noted that people at the edge of independence, on the cusp of leaving family and launching out into life, often retain as the other side of this independence a family closeness that is both more and less than family affection. It has some of the earlier coloring of the ties to parents, with its physical demands, deep-running libidinal currents, and heightened sensations. And it retains some of the egocentricity that marks childhood relationships: "they" exist for me. The individual has not yet reached that insecurely held feature of later life in which others are both separate from us and as important as we are to ourselves. There occur too such features of independence as arrogance and wildness that are easy to confuse with an earlier time of life. Thus the young person at the Oedipal cusp has a foot in both worlds, and so subtle and intermixed is the relationship between them that it is not easy to determine whether a symptom is a symptom or, instead, a sign of health and movement. Is anxiety really that, or simply excitement?

Just as hysterics—as the most vehemently articulate of the above patients were called—to a significant extent invented psychotherapy, so psychotherapy continues to discover itself in the encounters with hysterics. This is so for a paradoxical and disconcerting reason: hysterical patients are often more adventurous and mature than their helpers. Standing at the edge of new life, sometimes constrained by timid elders who are frightened to appreciate this new creature they have borne, the hysterics invite a rethinking of the conventional, a recasting of the old into the still hesitant vision they have of the new. It therefore behooves their helpers, once again, to respect what the patients have to say. Psychoanalysis easily loses this respect in its sometimes complacent sense of grasping everything. We often forget that the arrogance of youth is a necessary part of young confronting old, whether in life or science. Freud set here, as in so much else, a splendid example. Remember what he did. The chief obligation of elders remains to make what has been learned interesting enough so it is not neglected by the next generation.

My young patient was very pretty. It was easy to imagine why so many hurried to counsel and guide her. Further, she presented herself dramatically, sometimes sensationally, with a full, literal disclosure of her varied sensations, so that any therapist had much to contemplate and analyze. She could even seem a little mad. The sober psychopathologist might suspect megalomania, exhibitionism, volatility, much else. Yet it all seemed to me mostly the high spirits of youth, combined with a wonderful, often teasing imagination. I had to remind myself of the perils of psychological judgment.

She came to see me because her mother, herself a psychiatrist, thought she needed to. The beautiful daughter was in college in a nearby city, had experienced one turbulent relationship after another, and was encouraged to "share" the resulting emotions with the mother. I suspected that each amplified the other's feelings because this sharing, far from calming the patient down, exacerbated her agitation and led to threats of flight, even suicide. I noted, however, that all through these whirlwinds, the patient went on her very successful academic way.

I also noted that, even at her most volatile, there was an important corrective tendency in her associations. "I can't go on," she would cry out, and then a little later, "There is a paper I must finish on Monday." "I can't imagine a future without Carl," and five minutes later came the description of a new interest. The corrections were often immediate and trenchant; she never left the earth for long. I took this to mean that her self-reflective capacity was strong, that even the most intense feelings or extravagant fantasies did not overwhelm her capacity to apply reason, sustain a judgment, even calm herself down, unless (and this is a critical "unless") someone she trusted did not collude in her excitement. I quickly saw that my job was in part to maintain an emotional neutrality that could not be set afire.

There was one more significant feature of her associations: she "triangulated," over and over again. If she mentioned a boyfriend, one of his past loves soon appeared. Discussion of mother led to father. The pattern of her mental reflections was three-part, seldom the patient and only one other person. I have come to trust this as a sign of a basically stabilized inner life. It has often been claimed that triangulation means the patient's development has incorporated a secure family experience that anchors mental life. It may also explain the self-correcting tendency I have just remarked on: no one voice speaks alone. As is true of lucky families, each spouse brings a note of sanity and correction to the utterances of the other. Perhaps this was now a firm part of her selfhood.

So I felt free to settle down and listen. I used Freud's invention, which seemed just right for this patient. I became removed, largely anonymous and silent, spoke only to elicit associations, and practiced an evenly suspended attention. In order to grow, she needed to be left alone. But her compelling attractiveness, complaints, dependence, and uncertainty combined to make this almost impossible. What she needed was a device that at the same time captured her expectation of being helped and did not exploit it. Of course this is a "being alone" with someone, but that someone must leave her alone. We will see that Freud's invention is as precise as penicillin, and very similar in its mode of action.

This neutrality is not entirely what it seems. It is the emotional facet of a certain kind of leaving alone. The therapist is not neutral about the patient's making it on his or her own; quite

the contrary, the neutrality of silence can also conceal a prayer.
The secret prayer has been wonderfully rendered in a poem of
Richard Wilbur's, "The Writer":

> In her room at the prow of the house
> Where light breaks, and the windows are tossed with linden,
> My daughter is writing a story.
>
> I pause in the stairwell, hearing
> From her shut door a commotion of typewriter-keys
> Like a chain hauled over a gunwale.
>
> Young as she is, the stuff
> Of her life is a great cargo, and some of it heavy:
> I wish her a lucky passage.
>
> But now it is she who pauses,
> As if to reject my thought and its easy figure.
> A stillness greatens in which
>
> The whole house seems to be thinking,
> And then she is at it again with a bunched clamor
> Of strokes, and again is silent.
>
> I remember the dazed starling
> Which was trapped in that very room, two years ago;
> How we stole in, lifted a sash
>
> And retreated, not to affright it;
> And how for a helpless hour, through the crack of the door,
> We watched the sleek, wild, dark
>
> And iridescent creature
> Batter against the brilliance, drop like a glove
> To the hard floor, or the desk-top,
>
> And wait then, humped and bloody,
> For the wits to try it again; and how our spirits
> Rose when, suddenly sure,

It lifted off from a chair-back,
Beating a smooth course for the right window
And clearing the sill of the world.

It is always a matter, my darling,
Of life or death, as I had forgotten. I wish
What I wished you before, but harder.

In its turn, anonymity involves reducing oneself to a presence. The purpose is not to conceal or hide. I answer whatever I am asked if the question does not seem a distraction. The point is not to intrude: the patient is to be left alone. The failure to answer a nondistracting question is, in fact, an intrusion, of one's absence. This justifies what is otherwise contradictory in the theory of psychoanalytic work: the analyst is told to be anonymous, but in fact he is known to the patient by his appearance, his office, his very name.

It was, of course, the silence, this extraordinary listening, that set analytic work off most dramatically from what had preceded it. We will see in a moment that this listening has often been misunderstood. It was not meant to be the listening of a hunter, directed, impatient, intent. That would violate what Freud meant by the even suspension of attention. It is more like the silence of the night, all around yet incomplete, because wind, trees, and insects sound out; so the therapist's chair creaks, or the therapist himself, again presence not absence. Moreover, this silence draws from the patient, also expectant and waiting, the very excitement and hopes that have impeded the patient's independent functioning. The stage is set.

The evenly hovering or suspended attention (as it has been differently translated) represents the most subtle and crucial aspect of Freud's technique. It included not only the avoidance of formulating, reaching for meaning, or even thinking about any aspect of the patient's associations in particular, but a whole state of mind difficult to describe. Any description is your own; this concept lies at the frontier of psychological work. Thus directing attention means interpretation and intrusion when the goal is to allow the fullest, freest development of the person's own thoughts; again, the patient is to be let alone. But it is most difficult to describe what substitutes for directing attention. Perhaps the phrase "pure presence" will do—an accompanying that does not stay too close, an interest that does not itself attempt to be interesting. Freud emphasized one result of evenly suspended attention that illuminates the attention itself. The analyst should be surprised, that is, pure presence opens the way to surprise. Not thinking actively, not trying to explain or predict, makes it easier to hear the successive associations just as they are, still free of imputed meaning or connection, so that something unexpected, even unique, will not pass unheard because a prejudgment has excluded it. Now this is a paradox. Why should surprise be an experience of the drifting mind when formulation itself invites surprise by laying down expectations that can be violated? Indeed, can there be any surprise at all unless there is some prejudgment to run aground?

Students of creativity have suggested that the creative moment must bear contradiction. Einstein grasping that the freely falling body is also at rest, Picasso seeing at once before and behind, Freud suggesting that a passive stance might penetrate most deeply and sharply—it is the capacity to hold two apparently irreconcilable positions at once that makes these examples of creativity what they are, creative, surprising. This is not a far cry from those insights that give psychotherapeutic work its own moments of glory: it is a hearing freely.

One day my patient said she was feeling terrible. She had eaten everything in sight, been outraged at her mother, thought she might end it all. I felt some inward panic of my own, and struggled against the wish to do something that would quiet the storm. Most of all I found myself furiously thinking, figuring, wondering why. In very many situations it is hard not to think, and the well-trained professional person has very many thoughts. I believe it was Aristotle who said that anger is the emotion closest to logic. Certainly those angriest of patients, the paranoids, have a great penchant for thought; they too explain, and in that explaining put us down. So the generation of thought in my own case might be a function of anger. I didn't feel like evenly suspending my attention.

Gradually I quieted myself down. Here thinking was useful: I remembered how many of these tropical storms had come and gone. Thinking this way I was also not paying close attention to her and perhaps caught less of her excitement. When I came back from my solitary trip, I was surprised to hear her say, "As soon as I went back to the dorm and worked on that paper, I felt better." She had found the same solution that I had.

An evenly suspended attention permits opposites to coexist in the mind; the suspension of logical insistence permits even the most disparate elements to come together. I believe it is this unforced mingling that allows fresh combinations to appear and shed their light. Note that the process of discovery is not occurring to the therapist's mind—I was not thinking about the patient. The free passage of thoughts in the patient's speech and the therapist's mind occupies a space between the two; discoveries are not made by separate minds, but spring up in the common space. This is a microcosm of a greater cultural fact, that new ideas occur to the culture at large, often in several places at once.

Surprise is a result of random mingling, of the failure to impose a familiar or conventional grid of meaning, and of these two factors together: the real shows itself when convention is somewhat suspended. It is not that well-established ideas or hard-won truths will be abandoned, because they take good care of themselves, from force of habit and the attraction of the revered. The need is to prevent them from altogether overwhelming fresh perceptions.

What was she to do, stay close to her beloved mother, venture forth on her own, or wander between the two, as she was doing? Here again there was a temptation to discuss and decide, and here again the genius of Freud's invention shows itself. My interest, silence, and waiting invited her expectation that we would indeed discuss and decide. What other reason was there to be here? Furthermore, her natural, healthy reaching out into my anonymity, the fact that she was paying me quite a lot, my obvious concern for her, all these concentrated her hopes of a new and more successful parenting in the treatment.

Earlier I compared Freud's invention to the action of penicillin, another material that enters into a relationship in order to block a pathological result. In the case of penicillin, the relationship is between the penicillin molecule and the wall of the invasive bacterium. Penicillin first attaches itself to the cell wall and then prevents the cell-wall metabolism from operating in its usual way. So it was to be for my patient. The very psychotherapeutic elements that concentrated her expectations, the silence, neutrality, anonymity, and evenly suspended attention, also frustrated the pathological acting out of these expectations. She was accustomed to others' reinforcing her calls for help, her dependence, the conviction that she did not have resources enough to succeed on her own. Treatment required a method that could support her hopes while they were one by one replaced with successes of her own. I could not tell her she was now on her own and would make it, for she could only learn that by doing. If she acted at my command, it would be only one more dependence. Nevertheless, we wonder, why does any sensible person—and my patient was sensible—talk to a silent listener? One reason I have mentioned: patients like this one are self-centered, deeply interested in themselves; and they allow themselves this pleasure without the conventional hesitation affecting the rest of us. In addition, it's true that I was responsive: I listened alertly, and my face conveyed much. But there is a still more sensible reason for her continued talking. One of my patients, another bright college student, said it clearly. He had been puzzled for a while, then remarked, "Maybe you think I can make it on my own."

The treatment also required that she concentrate her expectations on me. Otherwise she would once again look to someone else to continue her dependence. The dependence had to be held in suspense, that is, half believed in, or she would not stay with me long enough to know what she could do. She had to be held in suspense because the victory must be achieved in each of the great territories in which we live: the body, our life with others, and our work.

She began to advance on all three fronts very soon. In the beginning she told of the puzzling relationship she had with her body. She loved it, often studied it, loved others' pleased responses to it, but could not control it. Or, better, she could not control her relationship to it: one day she would feed it next to nothing, the next gorge it. And the body's image in her eyes alternated just as sharply: most often she enjoyed and even treasured it; then one part, her nose or legs, would seem grotesque. She was especially prone to experience fatness, although her weight did not fluctuate much and her fear of fat never reached the extremes of a full-blown anorexia. She sometimes looked into a funhouse mirror of herself, the changing image of which reflected her desires, partial images of envied others, often an imposed glimpse of her mother, even her gift for caricaturing popular conventional images and distancing herself from them.

But the relationship with her body was more than mirrored. The body was also an object she both inhabited and could stand apart from. As a child, she said, she had not noticed her body as a separate object: then she was her body. Pubescence had typically created the new relationship, when her body had independently flowered. For one thing, she could not keep up with it, and it always surprised her. What would it do next, could she tame it, satisfy it, make it her own? Sometimes the starving and gorging seemed the wild gestures of a genuinely puzzled master desperate to manage the beast.

Sexuality both heightened her alienation from the body and retrieved part of her identification with it. More quickly than most adolescents I have known, she saw that others identified her with her body more than she did, that she could use it at once to bring others close and to keep them at a distance. She even discovered the extraordinary extent to which many men identify women with their bodies and hope to use the body's responsiveness to control the person inside. Early on she discovered that lovemaking is not only the occasion of alienation from one's body—when the body is manipulated for the control of a soul—but also of new identification. When love joins lust, there is an ecstatic harmony that is as much a harmony between self and body as it is between the partners.

It is characteristic of these wonderful young people who can truly leave home that the discoveries of alienation and renewed identification are made both at home and abroad. She gradually gained distance from her mother, but she also discovered and valued those things in herself that she knew were also her mother's. The mother too had a volatile spirit and felt deeply. Once this had been a bond between them, later the patient resented it, still later it became a memory and something lovable, almost a foible each could recognize and begin to control. It was not as if the renewed identification distanced the quality itself. It was more as if it brought it home, like a familiar piece of furniture good for some things and not so good for others.

I could say she "matured," if I knew what that meant. Often I know what it is supposed to mean: settling for the conventions and expectations of some group, or mastering a set of tasks, such as intimacy or autonomy. But how do we test for such results, when they are so easy to simulate and, more important, are sometimes set aside when a life has different or conflicting purposes. Just as conventions and expectations can fix a lethal straitjacket on individual differences, so standards of health on the basis of admirable traits ignore the way human situations can call up the need for the most bizarre qualities.

Instead I judge the success of psychotherapy in two ways. Does the patient's appearance change? Does he get new friends? What people may say to you about their treatment can often be misleading. Some must justify an expensive psychotherapy, or others want to please the doctor or themselves. Many cling to treatments that years later are viewed as tortures. My father once described a fellow lawyer in New York whose majestic name and eagle-like appearance kept his clients in thrall. Young lawyers learned he was easy game for any suit on contracts or wills he had made. But his clients, bleeding and bankrupt, swore by him.

But a change of appearance is significant. It may be seen first in a new gesture, the way a patient looks at you or holds her head. In someone known well, these unfamiliar things are startling. Some patients look better, less mousey or withdrawn. But there are patients like my college student, who lose their shine. Perhaps they have been too beautiful, too stunning to be real, and the extraordinary attractiveness is tempered. I like to think they no longer have to please so much. Friends too must change when a person changes. Most often what seem to me predatory or conventional types are left behind. Much of what passes for friendship, acquaintanceship among men, and what seems so common among women, one person using the other to invade or manipulate, these are replaced. The daunting requirements of friendship, so defiant of our evolutionary heritage, that a friend should be both close and open, are now and then met. The psychotherapist has also provided safe enough conditions for a simultaneous closeness and openness. The job passes to friends.

I said that Freud's invention was like a piece of great wit. I could also have compared it to a detective story: a suspicion turning into a solution that is sometimes a salvation. This is what happened here. I suspected she could make it on her own, that her complaints of dizziness, purposelessness, a kind of intellectual vertigo before any large piece of work, were efforts at recruitment or, better, casting for a play that if repetitious was always interesting. She was dramatic in the precise sense that she re-created her family drama everywhere she went.

The solution could not be simply an unmasking. I could not rise up from the audience shouting that the characters were only Mr. Actor, Mrs. Actress, and little Mary Actress, not the more gripping father, mother, and child portrayed. No doubt she would have found some way to make my denunciation part of the drama, the work of a jealous sister, perhaps, or a betrayed uncle. Or, had I persisted, she might have done what George Bernard Shaw did with his balcony denouncer, modestly joining the critic midst all the applause: "I quite agree with you, but who are we two against so many?"

No, the solution had to be an integral part of the play itself, a different and surprising ending, like the ending of a detective story. What makes the difference in a mystery is the detective: he makes it come out right. But the detective cannot rewrite the story, much as he likes to explain it afterward. He must use his suspicions to solve the problem, in this case much as Agatha

Christie solved one riddle by having her detecting person almost become the riddler's victim. The drama there was heightened by the nearness of the miss, which every psychotherapist can testify to.

A patient very like mine once asked a wise therapist what in God's name he was doing through all those long silences. He replied, "I am just trying to keep out of your way." That is not so easy. I described one panic of my own, and there were others. My patient had patterns of symptoms that could have driven a neurologist wild, or made the neurologist wonder how any largely descriptive psychiatry, any psychiatry resting on symptoms and signs, can survive hysteria. The greatest difficulty was that I had myself to deal with as well. I have had patients I loved too much or maybe did not love rightly enough. I kept wanting to do more, prove my helpfulness, probably beneath it all win their love. Somewhat angry, prickly types, in my experience, are most likely to turn the therapists into real victims because therapists may feel they need to prove their devotion. In Richard Wilbur's image, it is better just to wish.

The solution is a salvation for a reason that I think is little appreciated. I believe psychological health is little better today than physical health was two hundred years ago, when people die young or of a dozen diseases, as the very poor still do. We do not know the measurements of psychological longevity, but surely to be moribund psychologically is to lack imaginative freedom, to lose a living connectedness, to see the future as apart from present and past. Such seems to me the fate of many of our people even in their twenties and thirties. This is not to say that they are permanently dead. Perhaps the greatest privilege and joy of doing psychotherapy is bringing the psychologically moribund back to life. This is what I mean by salvation.

I am not surprised. If the thrust of Freud's invention is right on a large scale, then a person's reaching a free and relatively independent state must be exceptional. A suitable degree of holding back from the lives of our children must be rare. And rarer still is its accompaniment by prayer and hope. If this is so, growing into one's own remains exceptional, our people are poorly prepared for life, and psychotherapy remains the thriving business it is.

I did not tell her when to come, how often, whether to sit up or lie down. I set no termination date. I had confidence in her and wished her freedom. She did not abuse my trust, and when she was ready to go, she left. She did not need me any more, nor me to tell her so.

CHAPTER 3

WORDS
AS DEEDS

Wandering through a bookstore many years ago, I spied J. L. Austin's *How To Do Things with Words*. Could it be the answer to a psychotherapist's prayer? I had begun to grasp the uses of empathy, the effectiveness of Freud's invention for those who need to be left alone, and Sullivan's ingenious management of the paranoid. Had Austin found another tool?

Then a friend, perhaps reading my mind, recommended Joseph Conrad's *Chance* and this passage:

She did not answer for a time, and as I waited I thought that there's nothing like a confession to make one look mad; and that of all confessions a written one is the most detrimental all round. Never confess! Never, never! An untimely joke is a source of bitter regret always. Sometimes it may ruin a man; not because it is a joke, but because it is untimely. And a confession of whatever sort is always untimely. The only thing which makes it supportable for a while is curiosity. You smile? Ah, but it is so, or else people would be sent to the rightabout at the second sentence. How many sympathetic souls can you reckon on in the world? One in ten, one in a hundred—in a thousand—in ten thousand? Ah! What a sell these confessions are! What a horrible sell! You seek sympathy, and all you get is the most evanescent sense of relief—if you get that much. For a confession, whatever it may be, stirs the secret depths of the hearer's character. Often depths that he himself is but dimly aware of. And so the righteous triumph secretly, the lucky are amused, the strong are disgusted, the weak either upset or irritated with you according to the measure of their sincerity with themselves. And all of them in their hearts brand you for either mad or impudent.

Here was a warning about confession, itself so dear to the psychotherapist's heart. It also could have been an example from Austin's book.

The heart of that book is the concept of performatives: the use of language by which psychological conditions are immediately changed. It is tempting to insist that any use of language involves some psychological change, whether in speaker or hearer. But Austin meant something more specific, a statement that performs an action simply by being spoken, which in turn illuminates what I mean by psychological change. When the priest pronounces you man and wife, provided it is not playacting and the priest is in fact a priest, your state is immediately changed: your social status, your relationship with beloved and family, often your name. When the umpire calls the runner out, the runner briefly leaves the game; he is no longer "in it"; if the runner throws dirt at the umpire, he may be out of it for good. A doctor may pronounce you diabetic or schizophrenic and thereby change the way you see yourself (even if the doctor is mistaken). The point is, priests and umpires and doctors preside over those who elect to be married or players or patients, thereby shaping the individuals' relationships with others and themselves. The same thing happens outside conventional procedures.

Take the case of a paranoid person. Such an individual has the greatest difficulty understanding that you do not really consider him at all, much less center your life on him, in persecutory or adulatory ways. In fact, he hardly exists for you in any form. This is why confessions are so dangerous. They bring you alive for the other person, stirring capacities for judgment and derision. In other words, confession is performative: it immediately brings into being the state of being confessed to, in this same instant turning the recipient into a duly appointed judge. Of course, that judge is not a Chief Justice or even those medical judges we consult for a diagnosis. But the recipient of any confession is asked to judge. Few can resist.

Again, the patient's announcement of a paranoid delusion acts like a confession. He accuses you of persecuting him. Until that moment you had not considered him at all—but instantly you judge him mad. This is a psychological transformation in the same way that marriage is, because it changes your psyche or mind. The property of psyche I emphasize is the one that seems to me clearest, most exclusively a product of the psychological: the way we see things. The particular relationship that performatives bear to a point of view signals their role in psychotherapy.

The two examples I have given—confessing and marrying—are very different. Anyone can confess to anyone else, but not everyone can marry you. Furthermore, the content of confession is all but limitless, the marriage ceremony less so. We can therefore see the two examples as polar points of generality and particularity. In between are particular confessions one might make to doctors or the promises and contracts one makes in business. Austin loved examples of betting: I bet you it rains tonight, or I bet you the stock market improves. Once accepted, the bet changes the relation between the bettors—for one thing, they are both held in a state of suspense. Here too there is a great range of generality. I can bet against you or the whole state, as in a lottery, or, on another spectrum, I can use the word *bet* to approximate hoping.

In the last chapter I discussed a psychotherapeutic performative without using that word. I wanted my patient to be in the situation of Richard Wilbur's daughter, trusted and prayed for. My neutral, almost silent presence was itself performative because I carried that presence confidently and prayerfully. Without my being explicit—in part because of not being explicit—the patient experienced my presence as a form of confidence in her. Otherwise why not advise and direct? The confidence—based on my medical judgment—also included a prayer, a hope, a bet.

Again, I did not want to tell her. There are occasions when telling people you are praying for them is wise. I imagine the commonest instance is before a great task. Then the brave one needs to hear the prayer, needs the explicit performative action of being prayed and hoped for. (Note that this kind of prayer always stays behind—the prayed for are on their own.) But I did not want to pray out loud. Prayers lose their power if randomly or ceaselessly used, and my patient was only beginning her life. So I wanted to embody my hopes. This is the hardest part of psychotherapeutic work to describe and the easiest to feel. It is like the coach's body English when his athlete clears the bar: the coach feels it all. My listening body was like that, eager to pick up hints of movement, with her in spirit, as we say, all the while not trying to do for her what she had to do for herself.

I will soon describe a patient with whom that body language was undesirable because all his movements were backward or self-critical. There was nothing yet one could wisely get with. My college student was just the opposite, bursting to move ahead. Yet her accompanying hesitations and cries for help had previously elicited only more hesitation, so movement stopped. Her point of view included, "I should doubt myself." My performative or praying stance changed that point of view because, by letting her alone, I showed a belief in her. She saw herself as trusted.

All significant contacts act by changing our points of view, the way we see the world. That is why having extended contact with a paranoid or depressed person is so difficult and so valuable. Their expectations of being victimized or thought unworthy are strong enough to turn all but the most adroit contacts into self-fulfilling prophecies. My college student was again the opposite: it took very little, in fact my almost absent presence, to set her in motion. Later she said that she'd told a friend how much the treatment had meant, but could hardly describe why. In contrast, when the strong presence of another person has changed the way we see the world, we can readily describe that other person's presence, his or her point of view and how it affected us. For my own, probably Oedipal reasons, I love to tell the story of my father meeting General MacArthur, how the general made my proud and independent father feel immediately obedient, even servile. The proud man had seen the world in a way he could not have imagined, and it stayed with him. His telling me, in turn, changed the way I saw him, as he knew.

How to do things with words, how to change the way we see the world, I often repeated to myself, sitting with a pleasant, modest forty-five-year-old man (he looked ten years younger) whom I could barely listen to. Absent, very absent, I was, over and over again fleeing the scene, as if it were the scene of a crime. I felt ashamed of myself, but pulled back only to be drawn away again. It was just as hard to attend to this man as it had been easy to overattend to the young woman.

I was being driven away by someone who needed me. The patient was at no Oedipal cusp I could make out; he did not triangulate; he seldom made corrections except to criticize himself. The words that poured out of him were pitilessly performative of me: much as I wanted to like him, I ended up pulling away. He was like a priest with an incantation that can empty the church. I suppose if, in the middle of the ritual, the priest cried out "shit, shit, shit," he might do just that. But my priest did not say "shit," although he was curiously benevolent about people who treated him like shit. Perhaps that was a clue.

He seemed a very decent man, hard-working, earnest, and of the highest ideals. In all the time I knew him, almost ten years, I never knew him to lie. Shaw wrote, "If you tell the truth, make them laugh, or they will kill you." My patient was not comical or even humorous, and I never heard him tell a joke. I take such decency and humorlessness very seriously. I have known many liars who learned to tell the truth, and far fewer truthtellers who learned even that measure of white lying so crucial to the social machinery. In other words, it may be easier to form a conscience than to lose one, perhaps because one's conscience will not allow it.

If so, the psychiatrist's job must be harder even than the priest's. I'm sure any serious student of either psychiatry or religion will resent the comparison. But it should be clear by now that I am no fan of such serious students. Someone once said, a Catholic I think, that religion was much too serious to be taken seriously. Our paltry human efforts to be serious fail before the real seriousness of ultimate concerns. Earlier I made the same point in a different way: unless things can be seen from different perspectives, they cannot be seen at all; and to see things from different perspectives is to see both how serious and how silly they can be. This has a significance for performative statements as well, because to tell a joke is not only to make someone laugh (what in medicine is a test and sometimes a treatment of the autonomic nervous system), but to change a point of view. Shaw illustrates that with his serious joke about serious people.

Not long after I encountered the serious man, I met, without knowing I was meeting, his lady friend. She seemed to me about as unkind and as funny as he was sweet and solemn. Later the patient told me that someone had said no one else could get along with her. The patient's long-time boss had a similar reputation. I present these questionable notations here to underline what may have already occurred to the reader. Perhaps you have remarked that I too have become a little nasty, even a little humorous. Again, had the patient brought this out in me, or had we found each other? What was going on?

It is a paradox of society and an affront to morality that the nicest people often seem the most mistreated, and some of the meanest get treated very well indeed. Psychiatry has a great interest in this mistreatment not only because we wish to offer a better course, but because so many of our clients find themselves in such situations again and again. I remember a public-health doctor describing psychotherapists as pulling the drowning bodies out of the river of life downstream, without ever wondering who was throwing them wholesale into the river upstream. To some extent, all medicine lives off the unlucky. Fortunately for general medicine, the prospect of death renders even the luckiest wary of their luck. But the concept of psychological death is not yet so accepted that the lucky see much point to psychiatry.

My patient was kind toward those who criticized him. Sometimes he found himself thanking people who said nasty things, and no doubt this reinforced their behavior. I know I actively had to restrain myself and still heard unpleasant things coming out of my mouth. Once in the treatment, when the patient's behavior had changed enough so that he could call me on my mistakes, he said I had hurt his feelings. I had called him stubborn, probably meaning that he shouldn't agree so consistently with his critics. But it didn't come out that way—I had simply joined his critics.

Earlier, though, there were no complaints. He did not see himself as victimized. This is another of those paradoxes of self-scrutiny. Some people who see themselves as victimized often make sure they're not, but my patient appeared thankful for whatever he got. He ate, as they say, what was put in front of him. God knows he had come by that habit honestly. Reared (that is the right word) in a series of foster homes, he had no chance for a permanent home because his mother kept reappearing, chiefly, he said, to criticize his behavior, and then disappearing. A bright boy, he soon discovered that people love gratitude, especially enthusiastic gratitude. He had exercised that awareness under some very trying circumstances.

The largest temptation he offered me for criticism concerned "understanding" him. I have termed his habit of thankfulness a habit. More fashionably I could have called it an adaptation or a defense, specifically a reaction formation against hostility or a denial of actual life events. In the formulation of one psychoanalytical school, he occupied the "depressive position," taking badness on himself and idealizing others. In this way he could preserve his desperately sought relationships with those others. A theorist of the instincts might say he was turning his death wish on himself or being consumed with masochism. I could have also made the point in an existential manner: that he had lost himself in a frantic effort at survival and betrayed his own purposes for the sake of placating others. No doubt he would have received any or all of this bad news with his usual thankfulness.

Certainly understanding must inform treatment, as physics does engineering or biology medical therapeutics, but they are not one and the same. In psychiatry and psychoanalysis the two

lie far apart: many often powerful therapeutic devices are little understood (short-term work, electric convulsive treatment,
lithium), and penetrating explanations await the means to apply
them. Psychoanalysis has consistently defended the importance
of fantasies in understanding mental life, what might better be
termed "neurotic convictions": deep-running beliefs about the
nature of oneself and the world, often partly conscious but also
below awareness, coloring the way we see the world. I call them
"neurotic" because they often hold us in painful patterns, however logically arrived at. I could just as well have called them
"characterological" because of the way they inform our habitual
actions. "Fantasy" refers to a single component, the mental
image or set of ideas by which convictions may be expressed.
But the word also unwisely suggests these are merely fantasies
and not reflections of what may actually have happened. One
patient dreamed of being a small boy alone on a barren tundra,
devouring the only thing there was to eat, his own arm. This
vivid image appeared like lightning in a night of bland associations. The trouble was, clearly seeing this, even knowing how
deeply he felt and how accurately the dream reflected his early
experience of having only himself to live on, did not change
him. It was still the way he saw the world, the way he lived the
world.

There was an even greater difficulty in bringing neurotic convictions to my thankful patient's attention. He would be further
humiliated. He didn't need to know there was more wrong with
him than he already felt, and perhaps something more profoundly wrong. The truth cannot make us free unless we are
strong enough to face it. Shaw was right: tell people the bald
truth and you might get killed. My patient might have killed
himself.

What I thought I knew of his convictions, his drives and defenses, his diminished sense of self, profited him only at one

remove, the way a motorist is helped by the bridge builder's knowledge of materials and stresses. In fact, I wanted to build him a bridge out of the desolate country of thankless unentitlement into a land sensibly honoring and thanking him. I intended to take him there because he deserved to be there, not because he knew the territory or chose to go. This is an oddity of psychotherapy. He arrived at my doorstep because he felt stuck and confused; he was not sure he deserved anything else. The same oddity afflicts medicine and surgery. You come to the doctor with an ache in the chest or head only to discover that a vessel you didn't know you had has been playing tricks in your leg; you may resent all that attention to your leg.

My patient deserved to be in the new land because he was alive. This is one way of saying that a healthy body and a healthy mind are entitlements, however much they have been denied by circumstances or individual mistakes. It is the grandeur of healing to look to your healthiness and not to punish you for mistakes, sins, or crimes (unless the treatment itself can be called a punishment). This often pits medicine and psychiatry against the law or social policy or even morality. Therapists must be enthusiastic about life in the same way that judges are enthusiastic about justice, or priests about godliness. The conflict is most obvious when judges sentence people to death or when priests condemn souls to eternal hell and damnation.

It is the ability to see health amid sickness that gets the treatment under way. Surgeons, for example, do not operate unless there are sufficient signs of life. Happily for surgeons and internists, they have noted an impressive number of signs of life, from pulses to potassiums, from electrical activity in the brain and muscles to the end products in a drop of urine. The great bulk of medical calculations are calculations of health. We in psychiatry are not so fortunate: there are few if any tests of healthy mind or spirit. Freud spoke of the ability to love and work. Existentialists wrote of affective attunement, imaginative freedom, the ability to tolerate death and the random. Erik Erikson wrote of intimacy, autonomy, and generative abilities. The problem is that we have no clear, quantitative tests of these conditions, like the rate of respiration or the range of motion in a limb. The result is a morbid outlook on even healthy people, a tendency to look for hidden problems rather than hidden strengths. The whole field is in the untenable position of attempting to define sickness before it has defined health. If I had a magic wand to wave over psychiatry and clinical psychology, I would call forth usable measures of health and strength, measures of capability in all the psychic parts and functions. Then we would know how much neurosis or schizophrenia someone had and where, not laying those sad words across the whole person like a thunder cloud, especially when we can't agree on what they are. Patients would be less afraid of us; we would be more enthusiastic about the patients. The work could start up quickly and strongly.

The surgeon cutting out a cancer decides which tissue is healthy, which is sick. In or out, he decides, like an umpire, and the tissue excised is just as out as the player. These are performatives. The pathologist may say the surgeon was wrong (he excised healthy tissue), as the instant replay may correct the umpire, but these second namings do not have the force of the first. Experts are hired because they are supposed to know. Whether or not they do know, they do decide. How about the therapist?

I was impressed by my patient's appearance. At first he dressed in a slovenly way that demeaned him, but his face did not demean him. He looked young, strong, and enthusiastic despite a rain of blows that seemed enough to destroy an army. I found myself wishing that I were made of whatever this man had. For example, his employer was, if anything, even more critical than his mother had been. He had remained in the job fifteen years, received every dirty-work assignment the company had to offer, turned each one around, had never been promoted and hardly ever praised. The shrewd boss had decided that this man worked best on short rations, like the old army mule. Here were the first signs of life, of a resilience, energy, and enthusiasm by no means ordinary. He did not see it that way. Indeed, I have never met a person so completely baffled by kind words. People vary greatly in this, from the politician's delight in praise to this man's bewildered dismissal. It said a lot about his experience of life.

What seemed missing from his psychic equipment were rage and sadness at his extended plight. I don't mean they were completely missing—I may have been reacting to their indirect presence by absenting myself. (Later I will present a more decisive and lethal example of that.) Nor did it take long to reach the sadness. Here the difficulty was in staying with it. Almost all my efforts to find language for his feelings misfired; the feelings were too far outside my experience. I was like a blind surgeon or a blind umpire in my efforts to locate, acknowledge, and validate what he felt.

This tenacious problem makes the most negative possible comment on the way psychiatry and psychotherapy are taught. The possibilities of biological life and organic disease are widely taught, as are the possibilities of unconscious life. But what enables the location of another's experience, a knowledge of the possibilities of human existence, is never systematically presented. I had to learn on my own that the mother of newborn twins faces a task of monumental proportions; she can be almost literally torn apart. Or that the death of one of a couple who are deeply in love destroys the existence of the other, often for life; as a rule, it is necessary for the bereaved one to obliterate every trace of the lost partner. In the present case, I had to learn "on the job'' what it means to have one critical parent who comes and goes, with the other parent largely unknown, amid a series of shifting homes. I learned the hard way, by making mistakes. Fortunately for me, others made the same mistakes, so that the patient brought out a growing anger at being misunderstood. One day he reported someone sympathetically comparing the patient's plight to that of a fellow worker who had lost her mother at a young age. But this mother had left behind a rich and moving record of herself that the child was early able to explore and make her own. This was precisely the opposite of the patient's experience, and what was meant to be a friendly gesture of compassion instead left him reminded of how different and empty his own experience had been.

Primo Levi describes the reaction of many people to survivors of the holocaust, that they should have escaped or revolted, when in fact there was no place to go and no way to revolt. Often our reaction to the unbearable and the unthinkable is a blind assigning of responsibility, as if by blaming the victim we can somehow distance this pitiless fate from ourselves: ''I would have been different. I would have escaped.'' In the case of my patient, to assume a pathological location (say that his genes or unconscious wishes determined his fate) would have been especially destructive. Did my patient stay with his unrelenting boss out of a need to repeat his earlier experience? Was he holding on to a lost father because it was the only father he knew? Of course this all might be so, but to announce it, to assume it, would be to throw down a fresh burden of guilt. Indeed, the patient already blamed himself in precisely this way. Once again, the psychotherapeutic point is not to assign responsibility like a judge but to effect change, to make possible a real escape, not just the accusation of a failed escape.

In my view, the healthy response would have been for this man to rage at his fate, not to accept it with apparent good humor or to seize upon his own responsibility. I don't mean that it would have been a wise response in his foster homes or present employment, for it might invite a still worse retribution. He should have felt his anger and revolt in the presence of loving friends or in the safety of his therapist's office. The absence of such a response was no evidence of sickness: he didn't seem to have any loving friends, and he was not yet convinced that my office was a safe place. His past experiences could only have convinced him that I too would prove erratic and demeaning.

I was able to make one remark that resonated with his frame of mind. Noting my own resistant and absent state in his presence, and the similar behavior he reported of others, I said, "Everyone tells you to get lost." His father, mother, boss, colleagues—it must have seemed like the whole world. Hallucinated people often experience this, a chorus of abuse that appears universal and inescapable, but my patient did not hallucinate. What he heard was there to hear. I had only to listen to my own thoughts in his presence.

He regularly left before the hour was up. I watched the clock. Was he reading me, was I saying "get lost"? More than anything, I didn't want to be like that. I respected immensely his courage, idealism, resilience, affability, and energy, and I sincerely felt he was a better person than I would ever be. Yet I was watching the clock. I hope he can forgive me if only because this was, I believe, the disease, the awful thing that kept happening between us, the continuance of a life story even at the hands of his paid servant.

Transference and countertransference are pallid technical terms that fail to convey the mighty forces that held my patient to his grateful duty and pushed me to speedy escapes. "Of course you suffered. Of course you have every right to protest—and now more than ever, at my hands, in the course of a treatment supposedly for your own good." I also wanted to say, "It isn't just my fault, you must be doing this to me,'' but I couldn't. When the blood spurts up into the surgeon's eye, he can't blame the patient. It was my job to offset this seemingly inexorable pattern.

I played with the idea that his unentitlement was a kind of personal absence, that I could not attend because there was no one to attend to. "Speak up, make yourself felt!" I wanted to shout, but any hint of that would be only another humiliation, reconfirming his being invisible, a nonentity. The only action on my part that appeared to have a consistently positive affect was performative: only when I played my part as an expert on human psychic health did I seem to treat him right. It was curiously like a naming, this naming of his health, like the anointment at a christening.

In one sense it was no surprise. I am supposed to be an expert on human psychic health, supposed to know which tissues are sick, which well, like the surgeon. So naming and acknowledging his various strengths might seem almost a commonplace. But, as I said earlier, his response was not commonplace—he quite completely turned me down. I was trying to help him take possession of himself, and all he did was make me feel that I was not in possession of myself.

Telling him that he was unentitled would be another sign of his worthlessness, so I spoke of his entitlement, how he deserved more from the world than he got. This he could not receive any better, which was perfectly logical. As long as he felt unworthy, my gifts must be handed back. It was only through the experience of my finding him worthy that his basic conviction very slowly changed. This presented the greatest single strain on the work. Any impatience I felt with his persistent convictions was felt as confirming them, so that I needed to be as happy with his resistance as I was hopeful of change.

The man also needed to change his job, since he had dug

himself into a role as degrading as his earliest experiences were. Again, it seemed impossible, not only because he was receiving what he thought he deserved but because he couldn't imagine anything better. Imagining or dreaming a better life means thinking well of the world, at least the future world. Long ago the phenomenologists discovered that many depressive personalities, especially those prone to obsessions and compulsions, experience the world as filled with dirt and shit (a finding the Freudian system predicted). For my patient to imagine a better world for himself would be unfaithful to his whole dirt-filled experience. He lived in shit, he swallowed shit, he felt his own utterances to be shit. This had to be fully acknowledged, with indignation at such a fate steadily developed. The difficulty was in his terror at complaining and the fear he also felt that to acknowledge a life of shit was to discover even more fully that he deserved it, that I would announce to him at the end: "See, yes, that is you!" Here was the greatest difficulty he had in the work: his hatred, once uncovered, must come to include me as well, not only for my errors but for my being part of his world. He had to be able to hate me even as he looked to me for affirmation and acceptance. Children do this in the volatile moods of childhood, but he was not a child and held himself to the most rigid standards of adulthood. The principal help I gave him was by expressing the hatred he must feel toward me: "Oh, how you must hate me, want to pour this shit off yourself, onto me," I said with passion. Of course he denied it. Of course he said I deserved a better patient.

Happily I persisted. My admiring his strength, his courage, his forbearance, his right to protest and mourn, bit by bit seemed to affect us both. Was I able to stay closer to him because there was gradually more of a person to stay with? Or was that all a theory to save my face? Perhaps I was simply not doing what everyone else seemed to do, demean and ignore him, after explaining him, which meant explaining him away. Or perhaps he felt better about himself, as the phrase is, because I talked better and better about him. I like to think I was doing a doctor's job, naming and establishing his health, and that it was effective precisely because I was a doctor, an expert on health and sickness.

I also like to think I was giving him freedom. Of course freedom is one of those things you also must take in order to have. But taking freedom requires gaining self-possession, or else there will be no one to take it. Perhaps I did that, helped him to self-possession, making something happen.

Reinventing
the
Interview

CHAPTER 4

TALKING
TO A
STRANGER

The doctor asks you a question and expects you to answer. He confidently tests your memory as if ringing a bell: the mind seems a passive object or an open receptacle one can reach into and draw information from. He forgets that you forget, that you can lie, or that you may not know or trust yourself or him.

Instead, let us see the other as a lifetime moving past, a flying arrow or, better, a train seen from outside at night, with its lighted, swiftly passing windows throwing bits of action and personhood out to us. The stream of consciousness described by William James, still less the other's whole movement from past through present into future, is not arrested in an interview. However much patients reflect on themselves before us, that reflection takes place on a continually moving platform. The other is moving, and we are too.

I can say to the train, stop, let me aboard to walk through your compartments, ride with you a while, see the world through your windows. Or I may throw the engineer out and drive the train myself (society says the doctor must do just that if he sees the train headed for a cliff). But I can't really come aboard. It is a sealed train, sealed by the fact that, observe you as I can, hear from you about yourself, sometimes learn your feelings, nevertheless the most cooperative patient in the world must speak from a separate existence only partly sampled and understood even by himself. So limited and inaccurate is this self-reflection that some patients say, "You understand me better than I do myself."

The most elusive patient I ever knew slipped into my office, as if he could move through cracks in the wall. He was literally thin, but his psychological presence even thinner, and he never met my eye. I don't remember sitting with anyone from whom I felt more removed. The idea of finding him a safe place seemed utterly remote: safety appeared to be something he could not imagine. Years later, when he was happy there, he said my office for a long time had been a cool quiet place in which he felt nothing except a vague apprehension of danger. His was a vehicle so tightly sealed that even the windows were black; I had no idea what to do. Nothing could illustrate better the perils of interviewing.

I did not want to question him, to stop the train, search through its compartments and packages. This was not because he wouldn't cooperate. I sensed he would stand still, report faithfully, put up with the questioning officers' blunders, even brutalities, like a good soldier. But I was a blind surgeon again, a blind umpire, not knowing what was sensitive, what tough, where he hurt, what he enjoyed. I felt it would have been the easiest thing in the world to drive this man mad or at least drive him away.

The questioning investigator and the patient are pitted against a common enemy, most obviously when the enemy is in that intimate stranger, one's body, but much more problematically when the mind itself is both the target of inquiry and the examiner's ally. Then the startling capacity of the mind to be both subject and object reveals its paradoxical qualities. Is the mind under examination a quisling exposing its own secrets or a patriot, staunch in its own defense? It can be very hard to tell.

Psychoanalysis developed out of these difficulties. The skeptical Freud wanted to strike behind appearances to concealed pathological processes. He was no great admirer of humankind; he did not need Richard III to tell him that people, even the "best people," can smile and murder while they smile. Further, not only is the mind capable of deceiving others, Freud knew that it could deceive itself. It could not know, or at least be unable to report, much of what it was doing or thinking or feeling. It could be opaque to itself. Here was an element of mind throwing into doubt all the previous results of the study of mental phenomena. But my patient had been in psychoanalysis for several years. At the end he had been hospitalized with what he said was a psychosis. So silence and neutrality did not constitute a safe place for him.

The train might be stopped and searched, or one might sit behind the engineer, urge him on, faster and faster or farther and farther, in my patient's case dangerously fast or far. These two positions, fore and aft, have been the traditional positions in clinical work: investigators sit either facing or behind the patient. In this century two more positions have been added, one beside and the other more or less bestride. These stances are closer to the patient's movement, are less observing and more participating; both attend more to form and feeling, and less to the content of speech. They are both more behavioral and less intellectual than the traditional approaches. And the idea of giving freedom to the associations that psychoanalysis introduced to discover the hidden real is strengthened and rearmed for the many clinical situations in which the Freudian procedure is unproductive.

I wanted to be beside the patient, sitting or standing so that

I could watch out of the corner of my eye while the two of us looked forward together. I didn't want to stare and embarrass, nor disappear and leave him alone. Above all, I didn't want to center attention on a man who proved so excruciatingly sensitive and responsible, so quick to see himself as pathological and therefore undesirable. It turned out too that being beside was a "looking forward," which opposed his static despair. Optimism would have been fatuous, but a slight turn to the future might be a relief from the morbid inwardness that constituted his life.

So I did what Sullivan suggested. I put my chair next to his, literally side by side, not face to face but ear to ear. It represented the spatial statement of a psychological fact: I am on your side, we look out together, our search for trouble is more in the world out there than in you as solitary being.

My language followed suit. Talk was not about patient or interviewer but about them or it, the world looked at, where the train is headed. The screen on which the clinical picture took form was not the blank screen of analysis, where the anonymous analyst will find the patient's projected images. The screen was out there, watched like a movie for its emerging sounds and shapes. Sometimes I made remarks so ambiguous, like a projective test, that they drew out elements from the patient that hardly seemed related to the remarks themselves. In fact these projections, like an artist's imaginings, showed the world as the patient experienced it. "There is no seeing what it was like," I said to this man so quiet and tense I thought he would burst. It was as if I had put a tiny hole in a dam wall. He began to speak, at first quietly, in time steadily and at last passionately, about what it was like: a murky, confused, darting world described as people describe forests in which they have been lost and frightened. I could almost see it and he was not alone.

At other times the marks I put down, my remarks, were ambiguous in exposing extremes so that the patient could select those he was ready to explore. The classic example of this device is Sullivan's "Your mother was not an unmitigated blessing." The "unmitigated" sounds bad, "blessing" good. What was she like? Probably a muddle of things, like most people. But how does the son see her or, better, what can he allow himself to see? The marks become, like the dam holes, points of widening perception, letting more in, filling up the picture with details. Sometimes I will say, "She was just five feet tall." Of course I don't know how tall she was, but I want to hear the fact abruptly, unthought about, from the patient. "Oh she was tall, big." Sooner or later he might get the exact height, if it matters. I'm not worried about being wrong. Medicine and science are both rooted in hypothesis-making, gambling against nature. It may even help the patient to correct me and note that I am pleased, not angry. Once again, my elusive patient needed help in seeing that.

In the same way I steered. Here too there are fundamental differences among the metaphors appropriate to each of psychiatry's schools. The medical psychologist examines, tests, interrogates the patient as an object he all but holds in his hands. In psychoanalysis there is an extraordinary setting free, but all within the repetitive, couched, talk-restricted office session, the silent, watchful analyst sitting guard. The metaphor has shifted from physical object under examination to bird in a cage. The newer, interpersonal metaphor has a nautical or aerodynamic cast: the living object in flight or at sea, therapist nudging the tiller now and then or pulling on a line, the moving life uncontained, the forces at work not principally medical, investigative, or therapeutic but those of the world at large, like sea or wind. Marks steer. It is the difference between grabbing the prow of the boat, trying to twist it around, and pointing into the wind. "There she was, standing in the hall," I said. The patient is, degree by degree, moved as this new image comes into view.

The sentence subjects are all he, she, they, or it, the sentences declarative: the style is not interrogative, imperative (like the analytic rule, say whatever comes to mind), or rhetorical (like empathic work); it is plainspoken, error-filled, up for correction. The goal is to see what you would have seen had you been there.

But I'm making this sound easier than it was. Hour after hour I didn't know what to say. One difficulty I only suspected, at first, then came to know closely. His mind was extraordinary. T. S. Eliot said of Henry James, "He had a mind so fine no idea could violate it." My patient was like that. Every statement was qualified by his intelligence, rendered more precise, seen from several perspectives, the balance point of irony and directness often impossible to detect. My remarks went into a mental machine that rendered them half truths or, because of some implication unknown to my duller senses, disturbing to him or senseless. How I watched myself! Partly for this reason I'm not attempting to "present" this patient, to portray him. For one thing I came to feel that he understood me more fully and clearly than I understood him. Of course we seldom grasp the fullest implications of whatever we say to any patient. But this brilliant man challenged me to reinvent the interview, to show my thinking in extreme circumstances, how I tried to orient myself in the dark. Hence the value of simple statements, so much more like exchanges of gossip than interpretations of a case.

For all the down-home, would-be veridical quality of this work, however, something much more subtle and problematic lay in the background, just as Freud's search for freedom concealed his deep-rooted fear of the impulse, his conviction that only authority stands between impulse and anarchy; the goal of psychoanalytic freedom is to catch the impulse. What lay behind my interpersonal declarations and concern with actuality was also very nearly its opposite, a belief in the fictive. The meta-

phor of the sailboat or the arrow is a metaphor and does not
pretend to be anything more. The metaphor stands for the met-
aphorical quality of the whole task, what has come to be called
its hermeneutic nature. This is present in the understanding of
the very idea of the interpersonal—I adapt myself to my idea of
your idea of me, and so on down the endless hall of mirrors:
interpersonal effects are the result of interpretations of what is
thought to be happening, interpretations that of necessity give
birth to your ideas of my ideas of you. The fundamental rule of
interpersonal work, then, is this assumption of fictions. What I
see is a creation of the moment, a drama jointly scripted by our
various interpretations of the scene.

The excitement of Freudian work springs from the tension
between impulse and convention. The analytic procedure allows
this tension to be experienced association by association in successive conflicts between the freedom prescribed and the resist-
ing conventions. The analyst is literally drawn into the conflictual
field, being seen as the representative, on the one hand, of convention or of the fantasied seducer, on the other. The bird is put
into a cage whose walls appear to pulsate with the bird's flights
and haltings.

In contrast, the tension of my interpersonal effort reflected
actuality colliding with successive misinterpretations that had
concealed it. The "not unmitigated blessing" that one's mother
is emerges from this condensation in a series of details that are
what one would have seen if one had fully been there. This, like
the analytic transference, cannot be separated from the social
field in which it is reconstructed. The captain at the tiller is as
much one with the wind and the sea as the boat itself. All the
captain does is steer the boat. He does not propel it, and he does
not choose its destination if he is, like this therapist, hired to go
somewhere. But the steering requires some means of sorting
through the confusing signals coming from all sides. These sig-

nals reflect both the actual forces around and the responses to them on the part of boat and captain. My rule was the same as the interpersonal worker's: everything one encounters is a fiction until proved a fact. Every puff of wind, every wave in the water, can carry an unsettling message that might drive the boat aground. The various marks made are simply tests of imaginative possibilities, ways of stopping an interpretive development, testing its reliability, not letting fictions settle incorrigibly over an otherwise doomed voyage. So the patient decides that the captain is omniscient, a leader who can ensure the smoothest of crossings. The wise captain disabuses such nonsense, "No one will ever cross here smoothly," lest the happy passenger wake in fear or fury.

I wanted to be *with* him, not so much to understand his wariness as the conditions it responded to. We shared perceptions; we were like bystanders watching a fire or a parade. We could remain strangers, hopefully not intruding on one another until something like familiarity or the beginnings of safety appeared. We watched the conflagration as if it were a conflagration in someone else's life. For a long time this was as much ownership of his experience as he wanted.

The reader must be as impatient as I was for some grasp of the "material," as it is called, some decisive utterance or historical detail revealing the person before us. One wants so much to know. Traditionally this impatience has discharged itself in a penetrating question, an interpretation of the patient's resistance, especially accounts of the patient's alleged fear or hatred of the therapist. Here my comparison of psychotherapy to surgery must seem particularly inane; the surgeon has a reputation for vigor and activity far removed from the psychotherapist's. But a deeper understanding of surgery effaces the contrast. Before anesthesia, surgeons had their patients held and struck swiftly, to be in and out almost before the patient moved. Operations occurred in seconds, and no wonder: how else cut safely the writhing person? The introduction of anesthesia transformed the whole process. Surgery could be slow, and, as important, the time in preparation and recovery were not only greatly extended but made central to the remarkable process. The preparation of the patient, in the sense of determining risk, optimizing the patient's physical state, locating the lesion, as well as the immediate preparation for the operation itself—determining vital signs, putting the patient to sleep, relaxing muscles, cleaning and isolating the surgical field—all these make the actual cutting itself sometimes the smallest part of the procedure. And then there is management of the recovery, so regularly complicated by threats of infection, bleeding, cardiac or respiratory decompensation, even psychosis: the management of these are arts and sciences of their own.

Surgery was reinvented around the themes of safety and reliability. Interviews must be considered in the same way. My deeply wounded and sensitive patient makes the point directly: *do not cut into me*. When we see that the psyche is just as vulnerable to injury and destruction as the body, the comparison gains its full force apart from any particular person. We can't leap and cut or hold and question; we must prepare, prepare, and close up carefully too when the interview's work is done.

Often psychotic patients speak of "soul murder," and by doing so get themselves branded mad. In fact, soul murder may be at least as common as the murder of the body, though hardly acknowledged or reported. Again my patient offered a chilling example. Early the subject of merciless bullying, he had learned to hide himself through an elusive presence. I came to suspect that in his family the bullying took a subtler but still more overwhelming form: his mother's enormous and unopposed self-centeredness made every other family member a fawning servant. There was no space for separate demands or independent personalities. One could say that the patient had been strangled in the cradle if he had not been so carefully bathed and fed. He grew up envying confident bullies. He longed to join them, be forgiven and loved. This set the stage for murder. One after another of such "friends" tolerated his eager, responsive presence for a while, then turned on him or turned to another, and he was devastated. The result warrants the term "soul murder" because he felt dead, often took to his bed or obliterated his consciousness with alcohol. Still more telling, signs of psychological life were hard to find at such times, the psyche's equivalent of pulse and breathing. Sitting with him one would feel nothing, catch no expression of interest or protest, listen in vain for an imagination even slightly carrying him here or there. Amid all the forms of human absence, this seemed the least defiant or even retreating. For a while there seemed no one home.

In such situations suicide is one's first fear. Knowing so little, you work in the dark, and even a small misstep may sever the interest in life altogether. It is like surgery on the very infirm. One's first job is to feed the patient, rest him, exercise him just enough. The psychological agenda is similar. Above all, I wanted him to feel better with me, perceive a tiny crack of relief and safety in the horror of his life. There was an advantage for me in one particular bad time. I had seen it coming, watched this one bully's cruel enticement and rejection; we had gone through that together. So when the worst happened, I could make a move, from beside him to more nearly with him, to a first commingling of our reactions to an event. I was no more the stranger, bystander, spectator. Probably for the first time he experienced a fellow feeling with me and could surrender, if only for a moment, his elusiveness and isolation.

What we did was share a common human response. We each briefly surrendered the stubborn fact of our autonomies—each so nervously held—and settled in that imaginative and felt space. This is not the nature of most human contacts. What Proust called ''the first novelist's ingenuity'' consisted in realizing that what generally connects individuals is an idea or image that one forms of the other. This vivifies the relationship to the point of excitement in a story or of romance in real life. The novelist's ingenuity further consisted of simplifying his task and heightening excitement by suppressing the rest of the character altogether. Such I fear is also true of human life as a whole. It was true of my patient. He saw in his bullies only the glamour of their self-absorption; they saw in him a servility that, if flattering for a while, invited disdain.

It is at the intersection of lives that particular characteristics become important, often tragically so. Usually this is a misunderstanding. What each finds vivid in the other locks the two together, but then with some change of events or just the passage of time, the fit becomes less complete and the two are torn apart; once again they become strangers, and only then may one be forced to see the motives of the other. The selfishness of relationships gets hidden in the image of romance.

This is no less true of treatment. Clinical theories are like the novelist's ideas and images. They allow us to vivify a patient and to become potent in understanding. It is not that the theories refer to nothing real or important to know, but every theory acts to suppress, like the novelist, the real person who consists of much else. This is a central reason for the quarrels of theorists and the terrible sectarianism that still grips us. Medicine was once like this: everything had to be due to humors, or accidents, or the stars. If the problem of the interview is to open our ideas to as much of the patient as possible, the problem of treatment is related: one must be able to survive the loss of either romance or theory, to find some compensation in the ordinary for what first vivified the patient and ourselves. It is like marriage: what brought us together is seldom what keeps us there.

Some measure of safety is only possible with the transcendence of particular traits and the sharing of common ones. My patient and I had arrived at this point. But he had expected me to bully him; he had wanted me to bully him; this was his point of romance. And I too found in his mystery and obedience a certain comparable allure. What we had to do now was replace these different and potentially divisive attractions with something more ordinary and durable. It meant that the shift from being spectators side by side to being common victims of human life must be given resonance and dignity. The word is "moving," specifically to move us both away from exciting but incomplete views of one another to something both more commonplace and more complete. I could say he was brought out of his elusiveness to my grand openness and humanity were he not the smarter of the two and in several respects the more experienced. Again the sense of humor marked our progress and reminded me of a remark of Oscar Wilde's: "Nothing so destroys romance as a sense of humor in the woman." In fact he had more wit than humor, but it was equally directed at pomposity, drawing us into the commonplace together.

Even at the end I did not lose my feeling of stupidity and coarseness that being with him occasionally gave me. But I was no longer afraid. And perhaps the greatest difference between us might actually be his superior intelligence and perceptiveness, which I would be right to admire.

The interview is just beginning its clinical development. This psychological laboratory, entered every day by hundreds of thousands of practitioners and patients, has still to yield its greatest surprises. In such a setting, claims of understanding are part futile, part fertile, both folly and hypothesis-making. Our understanding of psychological phenomena is rudimentary. Indeed we hardly know how to define this thing—psyche, mind, spirit. It is constantly threatened by disappearance into brain, on the one hand, or into the psychic and superstitious, on the other: this ''where we live,'' which is at the same time central to experience and as scientifically elusive as the edges of space.

CHAPTER 5

RELIABLE
FINDINGS

A forty-eight-old man complained that his new employer was foolish, his wife emotional and unstable. He himself, after a major business failure, had just changed jobs. He came to treatment because he felt shaken up by the business failure and because he couldn't decide whether to leave his wife.

He had derogatory labels not only for the new (and old) employer and his wife, but for his mother and later his father and, less blatantly, for his last therapist. The patient was aware, however, that he might be misperceiving the objects of his contempt or that his expectations might be excessive or that he might be regularly selecting such unsatisfactory objects. He also wondered if he might not be inadvertently precipitating their behavior toward him. And he asked repeatedly if he were manic, having read about that condition in the newspapers; he recounted several episodes of mood change in the preceding ten years. All these theories were incompatible, and most had different implications for the treatment of his complaints, for example whether he himself needed to change, or replace, employer, wife, and therapist, or take lithium. It was easy to imagine how he might move from the practitioner of one psychiatric school to another, and perhaps to still another, until the correct source of his complaints was found.

My purpose in this chapter is to present the complexities of the preceding one in an academic, schematic way, both to rebut any charge of this book's having only literary interest and to render the means suggested for a safe and reliable psychotherapy more systematically applicable. I start with the issue of the location of pathology because it is a particularly vexing one. Each of the psychiatric schools searches in a different place for its pathology and often restricts that search to one place. The patient's responsibility for his own world is emphasized in much of psychoanalysis, and the part intra-psychic mechanisms play in the formation and perception of that world. Existential theorists (the position I called *bestride*) underline random occurrences and often see the world as more impinging than impinged upon. Interpersonal psychiatrists (*beside*) locate pathology outside the individual or in the mutually determining interactions called systems or fields. Objective-descriptive psychiatrists are closest to the analysts not only in their concern with biological or instinctive processes, but also in the focus on individual patients and their pathology.

How do we know which is right, and when? It is extraordinarily difficult once the sharp school distinctions have been put aside, for two reasons.

First, there are no measurements of clinical data. It is possible to suspect the occurrence of a great many psychological phenomena and not know their significance. For example, one observes what appear to be misperceptions suggestive of paranoid processes in almost every clinical conversation. Yet we often regard projection as a primitive process, even indicative of psychosis. One refers, of course, to gross projections, bizarre paranoid developments, or full-blown transference neuroses.

Nevertheless I think most clinicians would agree that there are also moderate degrees of projection, neither trivial nor gross. My patient may have been chronically and significantly misperceiving his employer and wife; or he may have chosen these difficult people and be correctly perceiving them; or he may have precipitated their behavior. Indeed there were hints that all three processes might be present in varying degrees. How was I to decide?

Some might argue that it was of no importance. The patient might need to improve his perception, his behavior, and his selections, and this could best be accomplished by a thorough analysis of his unconscious processes. Others might argue that the patient should be seen with his family or associates and their interactions studied directly. But surely, no matter what these competing points of view may recommend, there is one situation for which fresh means have to be developed: the situation in which the interaction with the therapist is at issue.

The diagnosis of mania is very popular today, in large part because of the eagerness to try lithium, and the number of cases so diagnosed appears to have risen impressively. My own judgment is that patients have probably not changed much, but that our sensitivity to the possibility of mania has. Fluctuations in mood, for example, are easy to discern in almost everyone.

The second difficulty of psychological cognition is this: the more closely one observes, interrogates, and tests a psychological system, the more one transforms it. This is obvious whenever you assume an unconsciously hostile attitude toward a patient and then detect signs of a suspicious and guarded person. The same process operates in the diagnosis of mania. Patients eager to try a widely publicized new medicine will be alert to any indications for its use; they may even exaggerate those signs to ensure treatment. In short, the context has produced the diagnosis. Furthermore, no psychological system is more exquisitely sensitive to such a process than that in which the observer is already part of the psychological system itself, and here we are describing interactions between therapist and patient.

I believe we deal with these difficulties of psychological cognition by making simplifying assumptions. I have just mentioned one such assumption, that of pathological location. An assumption of credulity or skepticism toward the clinical material also simplifies psychological work. By assuming an attitude of openness and willingness to believe on the one hand, or an attitude of disbelief or at least suspended belief on the other, the investigator more or less settles his position on the reliability of the psychological material. It is possible to classify many of the major therapeutic and investigative strategies by their positions on this issue. For example, the empathic strategies recommend a large measure of acceptingness or even credulity, in sharp contrast to the skepticism or provocativeness that is a distinctive part of opposing camps, such as Otto Kernberg's. I believe too that some of the theoretical disagreements between opposing camps spring from their different attitudes. This is because the basic attitudes generate some of the material that forms the empirical foundations of the theories, for instance the identifications and idealizations noted by Heinz Kohut and the hostilities and conflicts so prominent in Kernberg's descriptions. Moreover, each of these two points of view locates responsibility differently: the Kohutians with mothers and the Kernbergians with the patients themselves.

A third simplifying assumption decrees the superior wisdom and objectivity of the therapist. This creates what I term psychoanalytic asymmetry: the therapist's misconceptions (countertransference) are given less prominent places than the patient's (transference); indeed it is not usually clear how countertransference can be taken up in the treatment. The problem is important precisely because there is no compelling way to decide whether it is the patient or the therapist who is misconceiving.

Here, too, temperamental considerations are often decisive. Those patients confident of established belief settle in easily with their medical authorities. The least show of openness and flexibility disarms what suspicions these congenial people have. On the other hand, we have many, I suspect more nowadays, who are suspicious of all authority, quick to remember abuses of authority, and, at a more systematic level, often convinced that personal development (not to mention scientific development) requires a freeing up from authority, at least going one's own way to some extent. Of course the first group regards the second as eccentric or paranoid, and the second has its own characterizations of the first.

The fourth assumption is the most difficult to characterize and also, I believe, the most widespread. I call it the corporealization of mind, that is, the assumption that the mind is like the body in its presentness and visible contours. One often assumes that, because the patient's body is in the room, his mind is.

This assumption can be misleading. The patient's mind may be elsewhere; he may even "lose his mind"; and, most commonly, he may put forward parts of himself unrepresentative of the person as a whole. Also, it is often unclear how much of what someone presents is indicative of a personal individuality and how much is a function of the social field. In its most extreme version, social psychiatry doubts that personal individuality is present at all; perhaps, as Sullivan suggested, individuality is a myth, what today might be called a narcissistic myth, and social forces and shapings are the only reality. Plainly we need means of testing for the presence of mind and the relative presence of individuality and external influences.

My forty-eight-year-old patient was also troubled because he thought he might be in love with his secretary. He was certainly attracted to her and suspected she could make him happier than his wife had. But he perceived in her much disliked qualities reminiscent of his wife and mother. He did not want to go, he said, from the frying pan into the fire, and he feared a bitter and expensive divorce.

My patient made certain assumptions about his secretary that were curiously identical with the assumptions of the various psychiatric schools I have mentioned. He could, for example, be accused of corporealization of mind, that is, he assumed the secretary presented herself to him as she really was, that he knew her. He didn't believe that she presented only a small and perhaps unrepresentative part of herself, or that what she appeared to be was largely a function of his projections (I have noted that he was more open-minded about these issues in relation to his employer, wife, and therapist).

There was also evidence of psychoanalytic asymmetry. He thought he was in a better position to judge her qualities than she was to judge them herself or, for that matter, to judge him, perhaps because he was older and had hired her. Finally, he assumed that the negative qualities he observed were actually hers and not a product of his misperceptions (the assumption of pathological location).

Running parallel to these assumptions were certain equally dangerous ones that I might make. If I assumed his problems to be intrapsychic, for example, I might encourage a relationship with the secretary in which he felt free to marry her and correct his problems after a successful therapy. Or, if I assumed the love of the secretary was only another example of his mother complex, I might warn him off the lady and thereby miss an opportunity to improve his life. Nor was I likely to keep my assumptions to myself. The nature of my methods and investigative efforts would probably give off clear signals.

Should I take a credulous or a skeptical attitude toward the patient's material? On the one hand, identifying with his position and developing it empathically would in all likelihood reduce or postpone the hostile reactions so liberally displayed elsewhere. Such an alliance with the patient would be tempting, especially if I thought he might break off the treatment or become psychotic. On the other hand, a more neutral or skeptical attitude, while probably delivering the patient's distortions into the transference more rapidly, might also abbreviate the period of their resolution and reduce the possibility of the patient's feeling supported in his point of view. My point is, again, that we do not have systematic means by which to decide.

In short, a large number of possibilities appear, once the various assumptions of the schools are considered. At the same time, decisions must be made and, we hope, not arbitrary ones. That such decisions do appear arbitrary is attested to by students of psychotherapy, who often reflect: each theory or approach has much to recommend it, but none seems compelling—how seldom we penetrate to facts, how often to possibilities.

How can we avoid making these easy assumptions? The aim is to locate pathology more closely, to be simultaneously skeptical and credulous, to test for distortions, and to determine both the presence of the patient and the social forces at work. The price of this increased reliability of psychological observation is a loss in the precision of observation. Or, put in reverse, if we wish to increase the precision of our observations of, for example, intrapsychic phenomena, we do so at the cost of the reliability of the ensuing results. Concentration on any one type of phenomena, say associations, increases the particularity of those findings but distorts their general relevance. This is dramatically evident if the concentration on associations is so great that the patient begins to think about intrusive investigators.

The corporealization of mind. Psychotherapeutic work can hardly begin until the patient is present, "at home," and we cannot evaluate the effects of that work until we know what is and what is not artifactual. Yet we usually assume some element of individual mental presence unless the patient is comatose or has in plain fact lost his mind.

One day my patient seemed distracted. He talked easily enough but in a perfunctory manner, as if his mind were elsewhere. I suspected that in fact it was elsewhere, with his secretary who was vacationing some distance away. If I wished to bring him back, I had a number of tools at hand. I could wait, until his spoken words reached where his mind was. I could also call his attention to his distractedness, that is, I could invite him to bring a more active attention to bear on how he appeared to me and perhaps use that active attention to link up with his deeper concerns. Then I could empathically "go" to where I suspected he was. I could put myself with him in his deeper concerns by empathic statements, for example, "How far away she seems!" If this hypothesis were correct, he would feel me with him, perhaps that I knew his mind; he might allow me to accompany him further on that trip.

Finally I could deal with his distraction interpersonally, that is, explore the possibility that his leaving me was a statement about our relationship, reflecting the social forces at work. Bringing him back would then be a function of affecting those outside forces. It could be done empathically, by going where he was. It might also be done by affecting his view of me. If he, so to speak, left me behind when he mentally went with the secretary, it might be because he thought I disapproved of the relationship or was envious. A statement countering those projections might allow me into his mental presence. (As we shall see later, such statements can also explore whether I was indeed disapproving or envious.) An example would be, "Well, maybe a therapist wouldn't approve," perhaps deflecting the projection of a disapproving therapist.

How was I to know that what appeared to be my patient's individuality was an enduring presence and not an artifact of the moment? Of course if he had seemed psychopathic or hysterical, most of all an "as if" character or an impostor, I would have doubted his presence. But even in the absence of such suspicions I had to take pains not to type or fix him prematurely. Perhaps, for example, he was so pejorative because he felt something complacent or too accepting in me.

Everything is to be deemed a fiction until proved a fact; this, as I said earlier, is the fundamental rule of interpersonal work (and the opposite of empathetic credulity). The patient's individuality has to be determined, not assumed. The assumption is that, if the observer moves, the patient may be able to move too, to show other aspects of himself. By moving the observer, I mean projecting away from the observer the patient's views of him. An analogy would be to see the patient from different angles and thereby gain a fuller view. In the clinical situation the observer cannot literally move (in contrast to visiting the patient at home or in his work place). Instead one puts down different marks (projective statements) that prevent the patient from settling too easily on a single view; the patient is forced to respond to different possibilities. So I said, "Your secretary may be the one for you," meant to reduce somewhat his expectation of disapproval. He appeared startled, stopped the ritualized complaining and intellectualizing, and spoke warmly of how he used to love to run for miles in the country, away from his home and his mother's anxious fears.

Such interpersonal statements shift the patient's image of the therapist in order to test the stability of the patient's self-presentation. In other words, I can't know how much of his self-presentation is a function of his view of me until I observe his presentation under the impact of diverse views of me. Whereas the empathic method seeks to find the patient by the test of being with him, the interpersonal method determines the stability or enduringness of what is found.

Psychoanalytic asymmetry. I have said that projective statements are hypotheses of the therapist's clinical imagination. They may be ambiguous if the therapist is uncertain which mental elements the patient is ready to expose. They may be clear-cut if the therapist wishes to pick out something explicit for development. The point is that projective statements are offered for correction or completion.

They do not imply that the therapist is right—they indicate that he may be wrong. To acknowledge this is crucial. As long as the patient's misperceptions and misunderstandings constitute the exclusive burden of disclosure, there is asymmetry. And along with that asymmetry goes an implicit demeaning (and often heightened defensiveness) of the patient. It is not enough to reply, "The patient comes to treatment for the very purpose of having his misperceptions and misunderstandings corrected, and therapists are there to assist him, not to take time for their own corrections." This overlooks the two difficulties of clinical cognition with which I began. The clinical observer cannot simply note and correct. The material is extremely difficult to judge, and the judge himself may be deeply involved in the very creation of the material. And because each encounter has unique elements (these two people have never come together before), it cannot be considered simply another example of something the judge already knows. In some measure the interview is always a creation. It is necessary to acknowledge that there are two parties to that creation.

Even the reduction of demeaning and defensiveness is not the main value of projective statements. The main value is what they do to correct the therapist's misunderstandings. As a result, countertransference takes up an equal place with transference in the clinical work. When the therapist is free to say, "That may be the reason you came into psychotherapy," he exposes a hypothesis that appeals to him, for discussion by the patient. "Why did you come into treatment?" leaves the burden of disclosure solely with the patient, as does associative work; all that the therapist has exposed is his curiosity. The interpersonal worker even hopes that the patient will detect an idiosyncratic pattern in the therapist's offerings, which the patient himself can interpret and correct.

These statements by no means constitute a "sunshine law" for psychotherapy. The goal is not to fill up the hour with material about the therapist. As I remarked in discussing the assumption of mental corporealization, such statements provide a means to offset fixed ideas about the therapist. He must seem to the patient an elusive creature indeed. But, at the same time, his hypotheses will be exposed and tested. The patient can no longer complain that something is silently forming in the therapist's mind that feels like a secret judgment. Therapist and patient will now have almost equal access to that suspicion.

My patient spent one Thanksgiving with his in-laws and came away confused. They seemed warm, devoted to him, and even more critical of his wife than he was himself. He then remarked how similar to his in-laws' attitudes mine seemed. I felt an instinctive pulling away even as I realized that a bit of transference might have been exposed. But perhaps he was right, perhaps I had presented myself that way.

The in-laws' attitude, he said, was unfamiliar. Before they had seemed emotional and irrational, like his wife. He wondered if he had changed. Someone at his office claimed he was "a new man." He didn't ask what that meant but speculated that he was less obstinate and pompous. Perhaps the in-laws now found him likable.

I said, "They have some distance to go themselves," striking an ambiguous note about both their likability and his own progress. I wanted to see what would happen if I shook the amiable holiday mood, above all his account of my attitude toward him. The result was a short-lived blizzard of pronouncements and rationalizations. This succinctly illustrated what I believed we all suffered from this otherwise admirable man—and was one reason for his own suffering. In his relations with others he felt superior and entitled to be condescending. At the same time, he seemed a poor judge of the actual people before him and didn't engage them very closely. This was the judgment that had been forming in my mind. I was unwilling, however, to let it form too fully, not only because it might be wrong but because it would reinforce what the patient was suffering from. My judgment represented a superior, critical idea that might stand between us. Or, in countertransference terms, it might represent my own defense against being condescended to by him.

So I used this occasion to test the theory and, at the same time, to engage him more fully. "We're all more or less unsatisfactory," I said, and the statement put forward the theory of superiority, but at a moment when the relatives and I seemed to him satisfactory. I was calling attention both to the attitude of superiority and to the contradictoriness of his judgment; he was asked to question the extent of his actual engagement with people. But, rather than any lack of engagement being discussed and perhaps obsessed about with still further distancing, he was himself engaged.

The engagement I sought was an actual noting and correcting of me. What resulted was a careful description and analysis of my faults and his relatives', with his conclusion, "You're probably not so bad. Anyway I'm not looking so good myself." His later descriptions of his wife also changed, and he appeared to spend more time helping and less time criticizing her.

By engagement I mean a searching out of the object, as opposed to intellectualizing about it. He could not of course find much of me in the clinical situation: in fact finding me might substitute for his establishing himself in the real world. But a posture and practice of engagement were important for this aloof man, goals that clarification and interpretation could postpone, however much they mentioned his aloofness. I emphasize this point because the projective remark had two goals, to engage him and at the same time to test a hypothesis, which is an intellectual task. The technical problem was to prevent one from undoing the other.

The empathic approach to asymmetry is more direct and can be quickly described. It aims not at the correction of the countertransference distortions but at their temporary eclipse. The therapist is to disappear into the patient's point of view. In theory, by disappearing as a separate object that receives transference and generates countertransference, psychoanalytic asymmetry is destroyed. In theory, let it be noted, because no empathy can be perfect or lasting. At best we hope for a temporary putting aside of our personal intrusions.

Credulity and skepticism. The existential and interpersonal methods transform an issue of opposing attitudes into one of instrumentalities. Tools are provided for the full exploration of both credulity and skepticism. The credulousness of empathy, the radical skepticism of the fictive rule—these are no more than extensions of two serviceable but different attitudes into systematic means. I hope it is now apparent that such transformations are at the heart of my effort. I want to see naturally occurring attitudes or assumptions replaced by tools adapted to specific situations.

It will not be apparent at first how such opposing attitudes can be taken at the same time. Here I work against deeply ingrained habits of mind that are thoroughly rationalized as honest, therapeutic, loving, or whatever. One therapist "believes in" being compassionate, another in his objectivity; still a third that he can be both at once. The schools of psychotherapy collect their members, in part, by temperamental attraction to one assumption or another. The difficulty is that each of the opposing points of view are easily defended, and to a standstill. (The same can be said about the assumption of the doctor's authority). This is one of the roots of contemporary sectarianism.

The use of credulity and skepticism as tools rather than as "the right way to feel" depends upon a suspension of knowing. The therapist must accept that either or both may be right, but that he does not know. We could speak equally well on the transformation of a dogma into a hypothesis. The point is to take up attitudes freely.

The transformation of attitudes into tools or methods, with their particular rules, language, and goals, is necessary not only for accuracy and effectiveness but to facilitate learning. The naturally empathic person need not learn empathy, but he may need to learn skepticism. And many a skeptical person needs to learn empathy.

No doubt these remarks will be particularly offensive to those who believe that therapeutic work must be above all natural or spontaneous: talk of technique or method seems soulless, anathema. They will not be persuaded by accounts of the development of science, for example, from stargazing to telescope viewing; indeed they may feel that stargazing is closer to psychotherapy. Nor will they be moved by the analogy of dancing or singing, in which naturalness and spontaneity are the result of the most rigorous training and technique. I suspect they would be persuaded only if they could be induced to try, that is to enlarge their repertoire, just as those skeptical of analytic methods and ideas find themselves moved only when the Oedipus complex unfolds before them.

One day my patient complained that his secretary did not understand him. He asked me whether I did. An empathic response would have been, "You must want someone to," which might answer his question by demonstrating just the understanding he wanted. Or I might have responded skeptically. A wry "Who does?" deflects an expectation of understanding; at the same time, it shakes a little the right to such an understanding, derides the expectation as excessive or undesirable. On the other hand, "Who does?" can be empathic if the patient were more bereft and depressed than my patient was; a less wry "Who does?" then shares the feeling "No one understands."

I suspected the patient was brewing a very negative attitude toward me. (He had discharged a previous therapist in acrimonious circumstances.) I wanted to touch two partly opposite possibilities: his sense of being misunderstood or manipulated and his perhaps excessive demands for present understanding. He was at the same time wounded and hoping. An exclusively empathic exploration might frighten him by the resulting closeness and also prevent the mobilization of hostility that a fuller engagement with me as a separate person could secure. In contrast, if I worked skeptically and no other way, I would probably suffer the fate of my predecessor.

At this point I wished to be as empathic and as skeptical as I could, to acknowledge both the wound and the danger of the hope. And I didn't believe that I could usefully talk about either; he would distance himself by intellectual means. I said, "I hope so," on a rising, not too confident note—"But who knows?" In one breath I was expressing a wish to understand and skepticism about my success.

He then brought up what he said he had long postponed telling me, a dream he had had ever since childhood that recurred once early in our work. He was alone and entered a large, dark house, wandered through corridors until he found a lighted doorway that both beckoned and frightened him; he knew his parents were inside and that if he entered he would be hurt; his mother would make his father punish him. He then said, with an openness and simplicity unusual for him, that he had previously felt I must see right through him and that what I saw would hurt him terribly if he knew; what I knew had something to do with his mother and his wife. But perhaps now I was, like him, only trying to understand. I said that perhaps the dream did make him easier to understand, in particular that I might use what I knew against him and that what I knew had to do with a woman.

Pathological location. We see here, in sharp relief, the opposition of reliability and precision. Empathic and interpersonal methods help to locate pathology, but they do so by a "holding loosely" that sacrifices precision for reliability.

In other words, one no longer assumes that one knows who is sick. The family member who comes for treatment is often the most flexible and insightful one and, if not insightful, probably depressed and self-depreciating enough to blame himself. Any treatment plan that accepts this self-blame at face value runs the risk of reinforcing the depression. In fact, my patient became depressed both times he decided to seek treatment (hence the impression of a manic-depressive course), and this did not recur after the possibly self-sacrificial behavior had been explored.

By "holding loosely" I mean that one does not determine a pathological location. No single course of investigation is thoroughly pursued, as it would be if one source of pathology or another were assumed. In my patient's first treatment, for example, his depressive feelings and ideas were assumed to be intrapsychically determined; a great many links were found between his oral cravings, their inhibition, and the depressive phenomena; and very possibly our work gained from these notations. But his mood was not affected; indeed it worsened. I believe this was at least partly because he had taken on all the responsibility of sickness, which further inhibited his demands. In short, the previous therapist may have unwittingly colluded with the very mechanisms he sought to correct.

In this case, and in many others, I have been astonished at how the therapist's simple willingness not to assume, his holding loosely, frees the patient for a broader investigation and in many cases, and most surprisingly, from the symptoms themselves. This was true of my patient's depression. I was surprised too by the rapidity with which many aspects of his Oedipal feelings then surfaced. At one point, the clinical field seemed replete with primitive material and threatening gestures; not too much later it showed features of the end stage of a successful analysis.

Holding loosely has had still another unexpected result. When a patient's difficulties seem a function of the interaction with other people rather than of their misperception, and when fresh means can be suggested for dealing with these people, the tendency to act precipitously is reduced. It is my impression that a significant portion of precipitous actions in psychotherapeutic settings is a function more of feeling trapped in a situation than of resistance to recollection. Again, too exclusive a preoccupation with a single pathological location, when other locations are contributing their share to the pathology, may result in undue stress on the patient.

How is holding loosely accomplished? The attitude of not knowing or not assuming seems central; it has the force of a fundamental rule. We also need to support the unspoken side of conflicts, whether social or intrapsychic, when there is pressure for a decision that may lead to premature action. Thus I tended to shift attention to my patient's wife or secretary whenever he put responsibility on himself, and vice versa. The various psychic and social elements are to be held, so to speak, in solution, or within the context of the work. Now we will see how this same holding together of disparate elements might be accomplished in far more threatening situations.

Dangerous
Places

CHAPTER 6

ANATOMY OF A SUICIDE

A great biologist and wise student of healing, René Dubos, once reviewed the development of modern medicine in these words:

> It is because the physician must deal with situations involving so many independent variables that clinical medicine has remained an art even today—an art based on wisdom and skill derived from experience as much as on scientific knowledge and reasoning. The skill symbolized by the gold-headed cane was not mere charlatanism. It grew in no small part from the physician's awareness—even though ill defined and often subconscious—of the many factors which play a part in the causation and manifestations of disease. It was the fruit of the Hippocratic flowering. Far from being hypnotized by the doctrine of specific etiology, the good physician endeavored, as Pidoux said, to close all the roads through which travels the pathological process.

The pathological processes that lead to suicide take many routes. Like the diseases of everyday concern to the internist, surgeon, and pediatrician, the event itself is seldom determined simply. The heart failures that occupy the cardiologist result from intricate convergences of diet, cardiac reserve, exertion, the effects of medication, and a host of other factors. Similarly, suicide is the final common pathway of diverse circumstances— no isolated cause—a knot of circumstances tightening around a single time and place, with the result, sign, symptom, trait, and act.

Much in the traditional teaching of psychiatry sets our minds against this way of thinking. We are told about diseases, when we seldom have more than syndromes; we are told about single causes, when we know only about nets of circumstance. Diagnostic psychiatry, with its brave talk of schizophrenia and manic-depressive psychosis, was modeled on the bacteriology of syphilis and rabies, the diseases of prepotent organisms, organisms that do sometimes appear to act as overriding powers, sweeping aside other conditions to establish their unmistakable diseases. This is sometimes believed to be the nature of psychotic states: the internal process, still unspecified, will mark its victims forever, drive them down the road to dementia or return again and again in successive episodes. This does seem the way with some cases. But the course appears far from inexorable when we take the trouble to inquire into its details. And the prognosis is remarkably variable in any large group of cases carefully studied.

The patient came to our hospital when she was fifty-five. This age and her symptoms quickly supplied the diagnostic name. She was depressed in mood (she looked it, spoke of it, and depressed the interviewer, thereby passing all three tests of depressive affect), complained of many shifting and diffuse bodily discomforts, was agitated in her motor behavior and preoccupied with self-depreciatory thoughts, and had most of the usual physical signs (constipation, weight loss, dry mouth). We could thus easily arrange her symptoms into a syndrome. This labeling procedure with its resulting diagnosis—agitated depression, involutional melancholia, or today's term, major depression—was no great achievement, but it epitomized the overall examination of the patient and also pointed our attention in certain directions. Above all, it warned us: suicide, attempted or successful, is another part of this syndrome. Although suicide is more often successfully completed by men, we had no right to feel safe about our patient.

The label also tells us what many patients were like before their depressions. The name for this premorbid state is "compulsive character disorder," and this woman amply fulfilled the prediction. She had been responsible and conscientious, one of the world's supports, independent, confided in rather than confiding, the lady who, at the party, passes around the drinks and canapes. (It is very hard to talk of a disorder when the outstanding qualities are reserve, integrity, and steadiness.) Uncomplaining, she carried great loads. Even her friendships, if meaningful and alive, were shadowed by duty—there was no one to fall back on.

Furthermore, major depression has, in most studies, a hereditary element. In her case an uncle had committed suicide, just before marriage, and a sister had been clinically depressed. The method of transmitting these inherited traits is unknown. It may be through genetic means, through psychological processes of identification with family members, or through what can be termed a traumatic mechanism: the incidence of losses of relatives in the early years is claimed to be above the average for such patients.

Finally, the diagnosis allowed us to predict that something had recently gone wrong in her life. This is a tricky matter, difficult to judge. Things are forever going wrong in people's lives, and at the age of fifty-five death, disease, and disappointment are regular visitors. For this reason psychiatrists have never known what to do with the "precipitating event." Some have tried to pin most psychiatric illness on it; others have given it only peripheral status. Recurrently, mental maladies have been called endogenous or exogenous, internally or externally caused, depending on how influential the premorbid happenings appeared. The facts about our patient were ambiguous, as usual.

Two years before, her uterus was removed because of prolapse. Relatives remembered a quick change of mood after this. One complaint the patient made was perhaps related: "I'm all gone down below." Six months before she died, there had been a second operation, this time for bladder hernia. The details of the bladder problem and surgery did not appear to concern her, however. Instead she ruminated about breast cancer. The surgeon, before operating, had pointed out an inequality in the size of her breasts; two friends had recently been hospitalized with breast cancer. Also she had read one of her nurse-daughter's textbooks, felt a node in her armpit, and thereafter could not be reassured.

During the postoperative period she was cared for by the nurse-daughter. Since this daughter appears to be a central figure in the patient's story, I must break off the account of her illness, which appeared to begin with the bladder operation, and move back two and a half years.

Three years before she died, the patient and her husband stopped observing their wedding anniversary. The fact was quietly mentioned, and ostensibly its purpose was to save money. Daughter and son were away at college; a great-aunt who had lived with them moved out. A year later, the patient's uterus was removed. Soon after, the daughter met her future husband and became engaged. They intended to marry in September of that year, but the patient persuaded them to put it off a year. It was finally postponed for two years, to the September in which the patient died.

All through this story one hears surprisingly little of the husband. He is as historically quiet as he is said to have been in life. In fact, his last act is a non-act, the failure to do something.

The patient described her marriage as amiable. Actually it sounded bland, remarkably lacking in passion, unless its end can be called an act of passion. Only one group of family facts stood out. The husband was a Catholic; she had been a Protestant, a social leader in her church. It appeared that her minister was angry at the marriage. She never returned to her church and never joined the husband in his. The family reversed a common American pattern; she stayed home on Sundays, and he took the children to Mass. We know that it is clergymen to whom our citizens go first in times of emotional trouble, so here was one less resource to fall back on.

After the bladder operation she became increasingly hypochondriacal. Perhaps partly as a result, another break occurred in her relationships. She missed one appointment with her surgeon because of a head cold; he missed the next owing to an illness of his own. They did not come together again. Perhaps her hypochondria was the reason; we found it exasperating, and others probably did too. Already it was a little more than hypochondria. She believed she had cancer, having gone from being obsessed to being deluded, a typical and unfortunate alteration. What made her management even more difficult (although superficially more comfortable for the physician) was that she felt ashamed of her delusion and was only too eager to discount it. I say this made her management more difficult because it obscured the persistence of the delusion. There seemed to be an eagerness to have this exasperating woman well before she was, an eagerness she shared.

In any case, the medical people began to give way to psychiatric advisers. Typically, this period of transition is marked by two approaches on the part of internists and surgeons. First the patient was told that her fears were groundless, all in her imagination (one of the worst places to have them), and next, when this had no effect, that she was "overconscious of her body" and this was wrong. Whether it is wrong, I don't know: certainly it is sick and, in this case, not a sickness to be urged away. Reassurance (as well as drugs given for several months) had failed, and then exhortation. Her depression deepened, and she was referred to a psychiatrist.

The family consisted of the quiet husband, by career a scientist, the wife, a son, and then the nurse-daughter, the person on whom the patient most depended and who, until her marriage, kept watch over her mother. Finally, there was the daughter's boyfriend. Why didn't the patient like him? She said he was rich and handsome—no, she said he was "too handsome." Did she mean that he was too handsome for the daughter to resist? Or that she wanted him for herself? The mother effected two postponements of the wedding but could not manage a third.

She vigorously denied that the daughter's intended marriage had anything to do with her state. What right did we have to assert that it did? The fact was that, except for a peculiarly embarrassing and isolated episode of crying, it appeared to have no effect on her. But we knew she had made persistent efforts to postpone the wedding, and she showed no joy in discussing a superficially splendid match; she was, except for her tears and a barely perceptible sarcasm, emotionally flat. It seemed as if she were not permitting herself any feelings at all.

This was her state upon admission for clinical depression. She was assigned to a hospital service and a doctor, who set to work caring for her. It was by no means easy, for she denied any connection between her symptoms and her life, asked only to go home, and politely but firmly resisted his concern. Such is one of the most difficult situations in psychiatry. Here was a grown woman, old enough to be the doctor's mother, unaccustomed to confiding, suddenly asked to share secrets with a stranger. She condescended to him, politely questioned his assumptions, talked about leaving—but he held on. Gradually she began to trust him and to talk more. She also slept better, gained a little weight, and seemed less depressed. Now came the first of a series of events that may have sealed her fate.

Her doctor was promoted: he went from resident to chief resident and had to reduce his case load. She greeted the new doctor coolly. It had been hard enough with the first one, and now she had to learn to trust a second. Nowhere in the field of medicine is it so difficult to change physicians as in psychiatry; continuity of care is a basic principle of psychiatric treatment. When cases of suicide or relapse are studied, breaks in continuity are found to precede tragedy after tragedy. How could we discard our own rule in such a dangerous clinical situation? Or if it had to be discarded, why was the patient not given a more protective environment, further medication, or electric shock treatment, which is generally agreed to reduce the risk of suicide? The problem is really one of vigilance. When the night is long and the day exhausting, if the pressure of danger appears to let up for a moment, the watchman will nod, wander, or turn his back on the enemy lines. I suspect it was this way with us. The patient appeared better: she had shown the ability most gratifying to psychiatrists, the capacity to form a relationship; her delusions were less prominent; and the daughter's marriage was imminent. In retrospect, each one of these favorable signs shouts out a warning. The apparent improvement was only part of her lifelong effort to put on a brave front, an effort draining her energies rather than replenishing them. Yes, she had begun a relationship, but how much more ominous this fact becomes when we remember that she also lost it. True, the daughter's marriage was unavoidable, but by that same amount her own forces had been defeated. She was now helpless, and we had not a shred of evidence that she was reconciled. Where was our safe place then?

If the first great task of psychotherapy is to form a relationship, the second is just as hard. Many an effort that survives the first falls before the second. This is the task of accepting what the relationship reveals, for it is only after the relationship has been born that we can begin to know the deeper nature of a patient's sickness. And we sometimes hesitate before what is learned. Especially when the sickness is one of hatred, jealousy, perversity, ambition, or passive longings, the receptive powers falter. What I am suggesting is this: we may have hurried our patient toward a false health out of disgust for something we felt in her, all the time unaware of what we were doing. Maybe what disgusted us was her possessive love of her daughter, with all its power to cling, deaden, and destroy.

One week after the changing of doctors, one week before the patient's death, the nurse-daughter married. The patient left the hospital to attend the wedding, "enjoyed herself," in her words, and returned to the hospital as the daughter flew off on her honeymoon. At home remained the husband and the son, but the patient's watchman was gone. The next days slipped by with disarming quietness. Symptomatically she was better, but, as the last week ended, three events occurred. The head nurse on her ward, the staff member closest to the patient, fell ill and stayed home. Her female medical student's stint in psychiatry was over; she said goodbye one day before the patient's death. Finally, the patient was allowed to go home for the weekend.

At home the next afternoon, she and her son were discussing plans for a picnic. The patient asked where the highest cliff in the neighborhood was, as the best place to hold it. The son subsequently recalled this conversation with dismay, but at the time it seemed the most ordinary question in the world. The patient had an extraordinary gift for making the special ordinary, of turning the remarkable into the commonplace and unobtrusive. Later that day she took the family car, telling her husband that she was going to visit her mother. This pleased the family, who thought she was better now than ever. She went to the highest cliff and, sometime that night, jumped off.

All through this her family slept. At seven on the morning of the next day, they discovered she was not at home. Later her body washed ashore. The family was strangely quiet, almost expectant. The husband said, "Maybe this is all for the better."

Psychiatric practice, perhaps more than any other specialty, rests on the empathic resources of the doctor. These resources are vital not only to the understanding of each case, but to its treatment. Psychiatric treatment consists, to a significant extent, of heightened receptivity.

Most people have had suicidal thoughts, perhaps even suicidal impulses. I suppose they are most frequent in adolescence, that breeding ground of emotional maladies of all sorts, but no time of life is free of them. The crossings into middle age and old age provide ample opportunities, as reality confronts our aspirations with too harsh a stare. The slow compromise, or even surrender, of our fondest hopes is a regular feature of normal human life.

Age is therefore a great advantage to psychiatric understanding, provided it has not discouraged or rigidified a person. The experienced therapist has the least chance of separating off some people or events as alien; he is the least likely to speak of the psychiatrist's patients as the patients of an alienist. He knows that the maddest madman is, in Harry Stack Sullivan's phrase, "more human than anything else."

Yes, more human than anything else, but on the surface not recognizably human, and it is the surface of people that we see first. Our patient was not happy about her daughter's marriage, nor was she ostensibly sad or bitter; her response to the event was superhuman or subhuman, depending on one's perspective.

If she had come to us and said, "I am unable to give my daughter away; I must have her; without her, life means nothing"—or "I am jealous of my daughter; if only my husband had been like hers"—we could have more readily understood. But it is the indirectness and the unintelligibility of a patient's reactions that bring the psychiatrist on the scene. We are expected to determine what the patient really means. Just as in a physical problem, the practitioner is expected to determine the lesion behind the symptom.

I am not implying that our patient's whole problem sprang from the relationship with her daughter, or even that it sprang from her personal relationships in general. But the relationship with the daughter was a significant part of the problem, certainly the part we saw most clearly. Even allowing for the many other determinants, we were obliged to use what understanding we had as vigorously as possible. No one yet knows the ultimate causes of diabetes, but no one for that reason would refuse the use of insulin to the patient requiring it.

What happened to interfere with our use of what we knew? The patient entered the hospital, gained the attention of a doctor, and then the concern of a nurse and a medical student. This momentarily consoled her, perhaps substituted for the daughter she was about to lose. She improved. Then we changed doctors, and shortly she was denied the medical student and the nurse. During these changes the daughter married. We never allowed ourselves full realization of the impact of these losses on the patient. We partially cured the case by a substitution—a kind of artificial or intravenous feeding—of the original doctor, nurse, and medical student for the empty spaces in her life. Then we allowed the patient to go without the feeding, as if the cure were permanent. We didn't pay close enough attention to what might be called her social nutrition.

The study of object relations, as it is awkwardly termed, has been one of the central interests of modern psychiatry and psychology. Harry Harlow's work on object deprivation in infant monkeys is well known. The powerful effects on health of attachment and detachment have been extensively documented. The detailed and attentive inventory of a patient's human ties is today a vital part of the management of most cases of suicide, as critical as, and analogous to, the intake-output charts so familiar throughout general medicine. The units cannot be quantified, nor are they readily judged, but they must be carefully estimated.

What stands against a safe estimation? Easily heading the list is the professional person's unwillingness to recognize his own importance. It may seem strange to say this of a profession regularly accused of vanity and self-importance. The fact is, however, that many professional people allow themselves to come and go among patients as if their knowledge and skills were all that counted, their persons not at all. One sees this most vividly with medical students, who cannot believe in their importance to the people they take care of. Yet we are the great placebos of our pharmacopeia, and the power of the placebo can be measured by the results of its withdrawal.

Scratch most people, and you will usually find one conviction: no one quite understands how much there is to put up with. Worries about health, career, and family, fatigue, regret, may press upon human nature universally, but only we know the full weight on ourselves. This weight is heavier in depression, even though, as with our case of suicide, the existence and pain of it are denied. However much they are denied, one can be confident that they are there. To reach behind a false, brave front means reaching that depressive weight and its accompanying conviction of not being understood. How much easier it is to take a patient's bland answer that we have no reason to worry. Our patient told us, "But I have everything in the world to live for," and we were ready to agree. By substituting false encouragement for squarely facing the facts, we allowed her to support us more than we supported her. Most of us are afraid that facing facts with patients will increase the suicidal risk. Not enough are willing, for example, to ask the patient if she or he is considering suicide, as if the question itself might bring about the result. Unless one's motives are largely and bitterly sadistic, it will not. Instance for instance, feeling understood and discussing what matters are powerful sources of encouragement.

It is not easy to encourage depressed people, and most everyday encouragement is not encouraging at all. It says, "Don't have such feelings, hypochrondriacal symptoms, or thoughts; banish them from your mind. I don't want to hear them." I am not suggesting that therapists go about their business with long faces, wailing with their patients against the consulting-room walls. I imagine that patients complain as much about professionals' sober ways as they do about their prices. But ignorant reassurance has contributed far more to suicidal wishes than it has subtracted. Too often it is a way of saying, "Take your problems elsewhere."

I said that we may have let our patient reassure us and did not notice the sudden object starvation because we did not want to. We may not have wanted to admit that there was still a problem beneath her outwardly acquiescent manner because we did not want her. In difficult clinical situations, when choices are not clear and courses of action by no means scientifically proved and directed, semisecret emotions have a field day. The doctor may say that this emotion—this object-tie talk—is all art and no science. A largely impressionistic field like psychiatry is like seeing in the semidarkness: vision falls victim to illusion and bias.

The anger that our patient secretly carried may have been just as secretly present in our clinical decisions. The contagious quality of feelings is readily observable. We speak of one person as stimulating, another as depressing, one acquaintance is exciting, and another we find ourselves eternally arguing with. Such reactions are not solely, or even largely, the result of what the other person says. Manner, attitude, appearance—the faithful servants of feeling—give their tone not only to social life but to the clinic and consulting room as well. Anger is extremely contagious, perhaps especially when indirect and semisecret. In short, were we reacting to her unspoken anger by becoming angry ourselves? This is the way with paradoxically quiet situations: the charge is buried, and one must look hard for the marks of its existence. And the search must be not only into patients but into ourselves.

There is an old story that very nearly sums up this discussion of suicide. It is a story about generalship and war and, therefore, appropriate to these remarks about treatment and death. It suggests a comparison between the general and the doctor, springing from the amount of pain and fear each has to bear. The French Marshal Turenne, watching his army thrown back and near defeat, was approached by an aide-de-camp, who wanted to flee before retreat was impossible. The general was standing very still, and his aide-de-camp asked, "Are you not afraid?" The great Turenne, Napoleon's military idol, replied, "If you were as afraid as I am, you would run away."

Here is the challenge of suicide: to stay with the battle and feel, and not to run from what must be borne.

CHAPTER 7

SCHIZOPHRENIA

Probably no term in medicine rivals schizophrenia in the amount of confusion and despair it provokes. One of the great mystery stories, though still unfinished, it is full of clues, rich in suspects, littered with victims, and intractable to solution. The police as usual are busy, but not impressive, and the Sherlock Holmeses on the case offer divided counsel. There is considerable suspicion that the damage represents the work not of one person but a gang.

Once it was thought to stem from bad mothers. Now it is all because of bad chemistry or genes. These fashions change rapidly. The fact is that we don't know what causes schizophrenia. Most evidence about the inheritance of schizophrenic psychoses has eluded simple genetic explanation along Mendelian lines, although data do suggest that at least the propensity to some manifestations has a chromosomal base. The results of the physical and chemical investigations of psychotic conditions have been promising and should yield improvements in treatment. Such extraordinary disturbances of human functioning as psychoses must have large physical components, whether as causes, results, or parallels to psychological events. Furthermore, antipsychotic medications are powerful instruments for controlling many of the symptoms, even though characteristic disturbances of motivation and social functioning usually remain. These disturbances provide a large field for psychotherapeutic action.

There is no definitive basis for diagnosing someone as schizophrenic, no decisive chemical finding, psychological test result, symptom, or sign. The more severe the symptoms, the more dilapidated the patient, the more diagnostic agreement there will be, for it was from chronic patients that Emil Kraepelin, the chief figure in the development of psychiatric classifications, defined the condition. Still earlier a French psychiatrist, Benedict Morel, had described the rapid onset in puberty of a dementia-like state with poor prognosis. (I say "dementia-like" because, right next to the delusions and hallucinations and peculiarities of mood and movement, there were accurate perceptions and comprehensions, often very telling; the dilapidation was seldom complete.) Kraepelin brought this syndrome, sometimes called hebephrenia, into relationship with two others—one marked chiefly by disorders of movement (catatonia) and the other by megalomanic or persecutory delusions (paranoid schizophrenia)—in large part on the basis of a common tendency to an early start and an unfavorable outcome (an outcome that twentieth-century findings dispute). Many cases were reclassified if the patients did not deteriorate. Hence the original name for schizophrenia, *dementia praecox*.

I have spent thirty-five years working in and around public and private mental hospitals of varied treatment philosophies, attending at general hospitals, in a community where it is possible to keep track of patients over many years. My conclusion is that progress in the treatment of schizophrenia has been very limited. One other statement can be made with confidence: in no group of patients, except the suicidal and psychopathic ones, is there greater difficulty in establishing a safe place.

My patient, a seminary student of twenty-three, came to me between psychotic episodes and was therefore free of the dramatic symptoms and signs that first called attention to his psychosis. True, he smiled and laughed a good deal more than the content of his remarks warranted, and he was responsive and agreeable to an extent that suggested fear. But his movements were supple and appropriate, he conveyed feelings, and his stream of talk was not disconnected or bizarre. He reported subjective uneasiness, especially about the possibility of another breakdown, had a vague sense of being freakish or incurable, but on the whole dismissed his mental troubles and accepted his family's attitude toward the illness: that he was easily tired, subject to strange episodes, but otherwise all right; there was nothing really the matter.

Human life in general is probably made bearable by this process of dismissal or avoidance, which we term denial. I wonder if we could stand to live from day to day fully aware of the dangers of atomic warfare, the chance of a car crash, or the actual approach of sickness and death. For the most part, the darker facts of average human life are managed by being put aside, suppressed, ignored, or substituted for with happy fancies more in keeping with our hopes. Like all psychological and bodily defenses, it can overcarry; the scar tissue may thicken and disfigure. Maturity is asked to strike a balance between facing and forgetting, bravery and prudence, which should make the rarity of its achievement no surprise.

The patient's acute symptoms of one and also three years before were described in the hospital reports, and the clinical details were summarized as *acute catatonic schizophrenia* (a term no longer in fashion). The essential ingredient of this syndrome is motor bizarreness: stupor or mutism interrupted by outbursts in the acute form and odd gestures, postures, and repetitive movements in the chronic cases. Acute catatonic symptoms are often the most prominent symptoms in the initial attacks of schizophrenia, but they seldom occur alone. Shifting, often persecutory, delusions; auditory and visual hallucinations; and disturbances of affect, particularly oscillations between flat or distant feelings and sudden, seemingly inappropriate outbursts of emotion, are generally present in some measure. The doctor's own reaction to these signs and symptoms should be counted an equal part of the disease picture. If not puzzled or uneasy, or even appalled, you are unlikely to be in the presence of catatonia. You should feel like someone standing before a half-trained tiger. The tiger appears to be gentle, but watch his eyes and the fibrillations rippling down the coat.

There are many aspects of a patient's acute psychoses that could detain us: the details of his ideas, the apparent shattering of innumerable links within his psychic life (whence the term *schizophrenia*, or split-mindedness), the sequence of steps into psychoses and then out again to relative normality. Many unanswered questions would remain, especially about causal links. As remarked, psychiatrists have sometimes put great weight on the events surrounding psychotic episodes. Today the fashion is more to see the events as themselves results of illness; the study of social events and various homely details has been contemptuously called *la psychiatrie de la concierge*. In fact, we are not even sure when the illness begins.

My patient had been symptomatic at least several times before. But the more closely I inquired, the less certain I became that he had ever been well. A "different" child, seclusive, obedient, with occasional violent outbursts, he was sometimes burningly close, more often distant and rigid. His social difficulties reached medical proportions in high school with episodes of excitement and mild confusion; he himself dated grave self-concern back at least four years to the onset of puberty. He had, in essence, several beginnings, whether from the social or the subjective points of view, or still earlier from the standpoint of his personality's perhaps skewed development. The physician confronting even this small collection of material must be thrown off his medical stride. How much, for example, is disease, how much personality? Morel claimed, on the basis of parents' reports, that his patients had been well before adolescence. This is no longer so often claimed, but no agreement has been reached on a related issue: does the disease spring from the personality, or is the premorbid personality already affected by the disease? This issue divides psychiatrists the way Ulster does Irishmen.

When nursing him, the patient said, his mother's milk ran dry. He was vigorously toilet-trained at six months. Once upon a time we pounced on these details, the way an internist does on an abnormal cell. But it seems unlikely that they settle much. Fashions in toilet training, at least among the readers of books by pediatricians, change a good deal: there are strict periods and permissive periods. As for the milk's running dry, we would like to know more details. Was it a sign of the young mother's anxiety? Did it affect her relationship to the child? We are, in short, now more concerned with the atmosphere of the home and its modes of communication than with single events or special functions.

The father was a keen, active man, self-effacing, eager to help, strangely confident and puzzled at the same time. His enormous success in the business and public worlds had been achieved through systematic hard work, starting very early in life with the responsibility of his dissolute father. He had married and then left his wife for his mistress: work. Desertions of this kind are among the most difficult that women have to bear. Anger at a drunken or unfaithful husband is readily enough felt and expressed, but the man who departs and then sends back a check or a Cadillac may leave his wife for a time satisfied, and usually deprived of her friends' sympathy. Some wives handle these desertions by establishing lives, if not lovers, of their own. The patient's mother was a preeminently good woman, and a dependent one. She could pursue neither a career nor a man.

It is likely, however, that the patient's mother did pursue her son, and for this she did not have to run far or fast. They remained very close. Each described independently the conviction of immediately and intuitively understanding the other; each was extremely solicitous, careful, and supportive. They were like two children huddling in a storm: she could not stand up to her imperial husband, and the son cowered before his more robust brothers and sisters. And each felt the need to make up for something missing in the other's life—the absence of a caring man from her life and the lack of strength and confidence in his. You will often come upon these secret alliances in schizophrenia, and noble purposes silently and stubbornly adhered to.

The father said that he and his son were on frank, easy terms. This was not a lie in the conventional sense—the father believed it. But in the patient's hallucinations and delusions, there appeared an impressively frightening and remote figure, one he fought off and at times adored, who criticized the patient or looked down in furious silence. The patient had an intense sense that this was an unfair master and railed against his hallucination night and day. In four years of conversation with the patient and occasional visits from his parents, I discovered that this hallucinatory figure was much closer to the real father of the patient's experience than the father first described. The father had been distant and critical over long periods, as the man himself later detailed. The ''frank, easy'' relationship between the father and son was little more than perfunctory gestures of two people passing in the night. I don't mean that the father was to blame for the illness, either in the sense of driving the boy mad or passing on defective genes. Perhaps the illness arose de novo, or the family situation called forth some buried psychotic element, or the patient and family created in their interaction what appeared as psychosis.

No familial assaults or seductions emerged in the patient's story. The one sexual liaison he did report occurred very quietly, in the cellar of a neighbor's house, with a friend of the father. The patient remembered looking forward to his cellar visits with a mixture of fascination and fright. He reported too that he felt closer to this man than he did to his father. One can speculate that the boy, in his early adolescence, willing to do anything to gain his busy father's love, did the sexual thing the older man asked in order to win his affection.

He was never popular or successful either as a child or as an adolescent in any of the usual departments of life—athletic, scholarly, social, or artistic. He felt cowardly and exuded gentleness and compassion, red flags for other boys to taunt him. Among the disadvantaged—crippled children, members of minorities, very fat boys, and new arrivals in the community—he had a small following, with whom he immediately sympathized and felt understood. Jesus offered him a reassuring example: unpopularity, suffering, even crucifixion, which in one form or another he daily expected, had their rewards, perhaps the supreme rewards. It may not have been a long step from comparing himself with Jesus to the more grandiose proclamation of acute psychosis. Perhaps his father's being a great man, joined with the usual childhood conviction that parents are larger than life, fitted in with his being the son of God. In any case, from an early age he wanted to enter a seminary and become a priest.

Each psychotic episode began similarly. He felt alone, alienated especially from his father, sought sexual companionship, found it, and then fell acutely ill. For a short period, generally no more than a few days, he heard voices, saw visions of God, felt alternately confident and powerless, and carried on a furious and outspoken argument with the divine voice. This god was the very opposite of the one that had comforted him in quieter times. This god was an angry, unjust, and brutal power. Later it reminded the patient of certain childhood images of his father, but during the psychosis there was no conscious connection with any family member. He thought of his family during the psychoses, however, in a different connection. He believed that he must protect his mother from his father, and that this protection involved a sexual liaison with the mother that infuriated the father. Again he defied his father, as he seldom had in real life.

The acute psychosis soon fell away and in its place came depression: self-punitive thoughts, racking doubts, convictions of worthlessness, a black mood. This lasted much longer than the acute psychosis, for several months, with attempts at self-destruction, and was recalled as the unhappiest time of his life. When he came to me, the last of these periods was over. Now he was as he had been between and before the psychoses—friendly, compliant, uncomplaining, and perplexed.

About the acute episodes he held several convictions. First he believed them inexplicable, bolts from the blue and, of special interest to him, secret sources of religious truth. The nature of that truth was never clear, but the strength of the belief was enormous. He had heard and seen God, and although this man was sophisticated and skeptical in most areas of his life, the reality of that presence seemed beyond doubt. Seeing is believing: when the visual and auditory senses conspire to reproduce reality, and when that reality has greater vividness than the pedestrian sights and sounds of everyday life, such belief should come as no surprise. I have observed this same phenomenon again and again after acute psychoses, especially when the content of the psychoses is taken up into the vocation of the individual.

For most of us, religion must remain a metaphor, its figures pale images and its ceremonies, at best, symbolic of something behind or above us. Communicants we may be, leaders or flock, but hardly prophets. For the making of prophets, a more immediate contact with the divine stands as the first requirement. The prophet must be able to report the burning bush, the voice of God, or the blinding light on the road to Damascus. If some belief is to seep into the hearts of his followers, his own belief must be vast and beyond doubt; his certainty must be strong enough to be contagious. Reality is not enough, but if the senses conspire and to them is added a heightened sense of reality, a sudden focusing and brightening, the seeds of communicable religion may be planted. It has been said that human belief and ritual, customs and religion, begin in dreams. Perhaps, but I would choose as a more likely starting point madness, especially hallucinatory madness in which reality is sharpened and deepened (as in great art).

My patient's madness did not make him a saint, although it did illuminate what we mean by a saint. He felt secretly special, but he was no stronger, more joyful, or closer to others than he had been before. Instead he felt more alone and more worthless. The fruits of his illness were mostly rotten, to be hidden away. Here was the first difficulty in establishing a safe place. Who was this patient? A treatment can hardly begin without a patient, but where was he to be found?

The difficulty was not only that he might be frightened or hiding. I have said that a patient's physical presence does not ensure a psychological presence. This one often felt nowhere, in the sense of having no place of his own, feeling alienated from his body and ashamed of his presence, so that the human experience of being located in the world was partly denied him. In a similar sense, he was "nowhen." Much of the past he was afraid to look back on, he no longer felt himself to have a future (except a future of repeated madness), and the present he tried to keep motionless, horizonless, eventless. Any attempt to find and contact him had to do without the usual entry points: where he was, his past, his hopes, events. And his safety was easily threatened by attempts to force an entry by questioning and assuming a presence, which could only shame him and provoke fresh pretending.

In other words, this sweet, fearful man seemed vacant and drifting. It was not so much that he appeared withdrawn as lost in a frightened effort to please and adapt to others. I imagined too that the whole treatment could get lost as he learned to pretend to like what I wanted, wandering further and further from himself. So I tried to begin where I thought he was, or in this case wasn't. I spoke of the feelings that regularly accompany drifting in space and time, the emptiness, confusion, resignation, pretendings, so like sadness but without the mixture of pain and pleasure often characteristic of sadness. "It must be awful feeling futureless, alone, at sea"—not pressing the remark, talking almost to myself, lest I be intrusive or off the mark. The goal was to be with him in the nothingness, so that at least he would not be alone.

I also wanted to go to the bottom of his desperation, stay there, and then indicate what he did not yet know: the limits of this desperation, its possible ending. I couldn't announce when it would end because I didn't know. I couldn't even say that it would end, for the same reason. What I could do was put the idea of a future into his mind, as a possibility, which in a real way I stood for; for a while, I was his future. So I said, "It's unbearable now. There's no relief yet."

Besides emptiness, I also had to confront the argumentative

fury that lay scattered about his mental life, briefly and uncomfortably present when he was not psychotic, overwhelming and terrifying when he was. (His sexual yearnings would be reached considerably later.) Entering this part of his mental life was like entering a country at civil war. Actually one could not enter his mental life because that implies a degree of self-possession he was far from having. Such may be the essential experience of these states: the person is more a battleground than a person. Thoughts and feelings roamed the territories of his mind, entering unbidden, seemingly put there by others, snatched away unpredictably, while great armies of feeling sounded out and clashed, armies most often representing good and evil, god and devil. Remission meant a distancing of this uproar as if the psychotic person had risen above the battlefield, experiencing the explosions and conflicts only faintly and occasionally. Even a depressive resolution seemed a relief from such tumult. Then at least the battle was clearly organized, all evil inside, all good outside: there was a kind of self-possession even if it was the possession of evil. In contrast to this, well-organized paranoid developments were a great relief: then goodness was inside, evil outside. What one gained in morale was only partly lost to vigilance and hostility.

But I wanted to enter the battleground. Where was there any safety? If I stood too close to mother, I was attacked by father. If I seemed to represent either goodness or evil, I was overrun by the other. He was at civil war, so there was no central government I could contact.

Just as I wanted to be with him in his absence, so I wanted to validate and amplify any presences however faintly his own. But he cowered, as he must, on the battleground or floated absently above it: he was profoundly noncommittal. Not cautious like a diplomatist, hiding his hand, or like a pacifist hoping to be left in peace, he really didn't know where he belonged or if there was any place for him anywhere. This deepens the meaning of his being unpossessed. Most of us who lack self-possession hide somewhere, in a convention, a cause, an attractive or powerful person to whom we give ourselves. He really seemed nowhere.

Still another way of saying the same thing refers to self or selfhood. He had a rudimentary, incoherent self. On the one hand, he had the usual drives or wishes as well as the usual values and prohibitions: they were only too evident on the battlefield. On the other, he lacked an integrative or executive mechanism to keep the various psychic elements in balance: the so-called mature ego. In remission, however, his lack seemed different. What then seemed missing was nothing less than himself, that signature of ownership or possession we call oneself. And this intuition gains special force from the possibility that the lack of selfhood was what made him vulnerable to psychoses.

I wanted to find him or, if that proved impossible, help him toward self-possession. In this I was aided by a fortunate circumstance. He showed two qualities I love. He was at once highly idealistic and touchingly innocent. He believed with his whole heart in the possibility of justice, fair play, and kindness. For all the stinging disappointments of his life, he was the least cynical of men. Moreover, he was trusting; others received from him the benefit of the doubt, or really the absence of any doubt, so that even people repeatedly unfaithful to him stood forgiven.

It is a great mistake to believe that paranoid people need to be more trusting. Psychiatry has known for more than a century that people subject to paranoid psychoses are often too trusting, in fact credulous, and that the paranoid periods may follow after a patient is disappointed or double-crossed in a trusted relationship. Eventually I taught my patient a measure of steady vigilance or mild suspiciousness so that he could pick those close to him with greater discretion and prepare himself for demoralizing surprises, since it is usually surprise that makes demoralization possible.

But I also loved his innocence and idealism. I could admire what at the same time worried me. This acknowledgment of admirable traits made it possible for him to perceive the traits, which he could never do before. And my very liking of them avoided any need on his part to defend them: the necessary little adjustments of awareness and diminution became easier. Moreover, I was discovering him, these aspects of himself revealed at first faintly and unknowingly. The discovery was also chilling. He wanted to believe well of the world, so the disappointments prepared by his innocence were also defeats for his idealism. This is a deadly combination, and the reason may well lie in a formulation of Freud's. The ego ideal, he wrote, "is the heir of the original narcissism on which the childish ego enjoyed self-sufficiency." He meant that the process of human maturation must transform the infant's cry, "I am great, I am self-sufficient," into the sensible and great ideals toward which mature people strive. The danger of combining ideals and innocence resides right here, for if ideals are subjected to ruthless and repeated disappointment, the energy and structure supporting the adult personality may be so shaken that the individual falls away into madness and megalomania. It was this formulation that guided the specific steps I tried to take.

He could not believe in himself as long as his ideals were shattered because he defined himself by these ideals and attacked himself ruthlessly when they were defeated. My acknowledgment of his ideals helped to restore his belief in himself. The civil war was little by little brought to a close. As long as he remained a worthless disappointment to himself, he had to be a battleground of the self-accusations and bitter counteraccusations that were so terrifyingly voiced by the hallucinations. But when I shared his ideals and admired him for clinging to them, when I said he was great for clinging to them, the bridge back to his mature self was put in place. If I could believe in him, perhaps he could too, leaving behind the infantile claims of automatic greatness or evil. The point is a simple one, however difficult to achieve: people find themselves in the meaning of their lives. Take away that meaning and you take away the possession of self, being one's own person. My theory was about the recovery of meaning.

The recovery had another result, perhaps the most dramatic of all. As he emerged from his civil war, as the primitive claims and counterclaims fell away, *he* more and more appeared. There was somebody home, by the intuitive impression we form—more assertive, steadier, a psychological roundedness that is as self-evident as it is impossible to prove or quantify. But I had another and still more difficult task before me. Until he became less innocent, he would continue to be frustrated. Until he knew better where to put his faith and hope, he was like a climber of rock faces without equipment or expertise. Show me a cure for innocence, I like to say, and half of madness will disappear. I had no cure, but I did have perseverence and he had a willingness to learn. The hardest part was again his idealism, his unwillingness to believe that the world is the tarnished place it is. I don't think he will ever be street-smart or what Sullivan called "suave," but he no longer seems so surprised.

My patient gradually exhibited a quality that may seem paradoxical: he lost a certain heaviness that once had been almost the only evidence of his appearing at all. I think it was partly a loss of the depressiveness that had clung so long. There also seemed less self-importance, or taking himself so seriously, which, however, had never been a constant note or even at the level of everyday life. Someone has said that angels can fly because they take themselves lightly. My patient was not an angel or a saint or even a great man, not like the Desmond Tutu I heard speak once, in these words: "My wife said we must go back to South Africa immediately. I asked her, Why must we go back? She said, Since we came to America five months ago, you have been made a bishop and then you won this Nobel thing. Every morning when I wake up I feel like I have been sleeping with the Pope." Surely this is a man entitled to take himself seriously, much more seriously than you or I. But apparently he did not: although Bishop Tutu lived in fear of assassination and had the loftiest of missions to accomplish, he could still see himself as just a little man, the butt of his wife's joke.

Is the lightness of being that Tutu illustrates the evidence of a shift of weight or value to an ideal? Is that why he, like the angels, could seem to fly? Is becoming fully human this movement of importance or heaviness to goals and ideals, leaving the person as no more important than individual persons typically are? Then self-possession does not appear to be either self-importance or self-denigration.

My patient gained a certain lightness. And he recovered his ideals. We can say he became a little like Tutu, an ordinary companion to a great ideal. In this he reflected what individuals hope to reach in the passage through life, once the center, even seemingly of the whole world, gradually to become what people are, little frail things in a large world.

Psychiatry's motto is not the one Dante put over the gate to Hell, "Abandon hope all ye who enter here." Psychiatry abounds in hope, both for the alleviation of suffering and for the extension of human knowledge. But the proper words to put over psychiatry's door are still not ones to quicken every pulse. For we must write there, "Accept uncertainty within, or do not stay." Nothing illustrates this better than the clinical material from a schizophrenic case. We come upon broad possibilities for understanding, but uncertainty dogs our every step. Of course uncertainty is part of the lives of clinicians of every specialty; absolute certainty in clinical work is an attitude only for geniuses or fools. But the level of psychiatric uncertainty is above that of most medical specialties.

Not everyone, for example, would agree that what I have presented is a case of schizophrenia. The good recovery, intense emotionality, and grandiose delusions during the acute psychosis suggest an alternative diagnosis of manic-depressive psychosis; there was, in addition, not so sharp a difference between the extent of his psychotic symptoms in some areas and the degree of his normal functions in others, not so extensive a dissociation among his mental functions, as to put the case beyond most questions of being schizophrenic. But as long as we don't know what the necessary ingredients of the condition are, in terms of definite signs or symptoms, ideas, defenses, life experiences, or biological findings, there must be diagnostic doubt.

It is the varied abundance of material that best characterizes modern psychiatry, that stimulates its disputes, undermines its diagnoses, and at the same time provides its chief opportunities for growth. Psychiatry is the part of medicine farthest away from settled maturity, as strong as any in observation (perhaps even the richest, considering that social observations are much better accepted in psychiatry than in most of medicine), and weakest in correlations and calculations. It is like an adolescent, disputatious, alternately arrogant and humble, strong, full of promise, inconsistent, able to see what others can't, even preoccupied with sex. Without it, medicine might well be dehumanized and have to abandon half its patients. With it, medicine has less chance of becoming an army of technicians narrowly focused on little pieces of the human body. But medicine and psychiatry do not form an easy family. Each must be periodically ashamed of the other, at one moment proud, at the next ready to break apart. It will be a sad day for each if they do break apart: the fate of a narrow scientism opens in front of general medicine, and a vapid humanitarianism might befall psychiatry. This is much like the alternatives that life put before my patient. Could he contain the disparate forces raging within him, or would he split apart and wall off large portions of his inner life?

Schizophrenia brings us life at its most dismal, unharmonious, crabbed, and confined. Indeed schizophrenia may not be the name of a particular disease at all but a multiply caused human condition, still awaiting division into manageable units. As such, it offers important insights into our understanding of life.

We do not yet grasp the laws, measure the units, or perform the critical experiments necessary to settle our disputes. We are at an earlier stage of the work, when the elements and dimensions of the task are just coming into view. But we no longer look at schizophrenia in the way, in Darwin's words, a savage looks at a ship, as something wholly beyond comprehension. There *is* order and understanding, even if it is far from complete. And

when we regard every production of nature as one which has had a long history; when we contemplate every complex structure and instinct as a summing up of many contrivances, each useful to the possessor, in the same way as any great mechanical invention is the summing up of the labour, the experience, the reason, and even the blunders of numerous workmen; when we thus view each organic being, how far more interesting—I speak from experience—does the study of natural history become!

What Darwin wrote in *The Origin of Species* about understanding natural history could be written today about understanding human nature, whether in its more normal aspects or in its most pathological forms.

CHAPTER 8

PSYCHOPATHY

Schizophrenia provokes apathy or confusion in the observer; suicide causes feelings of guilt and secret anger. Psychopathy, in marked contrast, provokes many feelings, notably contempt and fury. Psychiatry itself is resented for approaching criminal behavior as a medical problem, for allowing the profession to enter an area that many regard as best left to policemen, courts, and prisons, to the punitive and protective agencies of society. Yet this very society, angry but at the same time wishing to help, administers medical aid to the psychopathic and attempts to transform its own disciplinary institutions into corrective ones, in the hope that observation, diagnosis, and treatment can succeed where jails and judges have failed.

This vast topic, which embraces ethics, law, social theory, and criminology, defies compression. At the turn of the century, psychopathy referred to all pathological behavior and mentation. It was not until much later that a syndrome took shape and a start was made toward etiology and treatment. The professional criminal and juvenile delinquent stand nearby, tenuously related to the main syndrome. Something more precise has come to be meant by psychopathy, but precisely what?

Emerson referred to a man who never said anything right or did anything wrong. This chapter is about those who rarely say anything wrong or do anything right. The sickness is in the actions, which give the syndrome one of its many labels. What the patients do is "antisocial" or "sociopathic," their actions striking against law, propriety, or the values and feelings of other people. One hundred and eighty years ago Benjamin Rush discussed four principal symptoms of "moral disease in the will": murder, theft, dishonesty, and drunkenness. Many neurologic and psychiatric conditions announce themselves through acts, such as the fits of epilepsy, the movements of Parkinsonism, catatonic mannerisms, depressive agitation, or manic restlessness. The first suspicion of psychopathy, however, is not elicited by the suddenness, rigidity, peculiarity, or speed of the actions, but by their seeming wrong or bad.

A man of twenty, who looked older, was caught trying to cash bad checks. His two rich maiden aunts insisted that he see a psychiatrist. For a while he only pretended to be my patient, regaining the trust of his aunts and some of their money. He achieved this with the same poised and winning confidence that he used in the incidents leading to his arrest. My patient had a magnetic social charm. It seemed a cruel rudeness to deal honestly with him, and he always had explanations that made it easy to forgive. Many felt privileged when he smiled at them.

This reveals the primary obstacle to recognizing psychopathy. If the patient is anything but an awkward member of his tribe, the thought of psychopathy never crosses the observer's mind. The psychopathic person can enter a bank, cash an unfamiliar check, and depart without kindling the slightest suspicion, even if the check is not his, the account without money, and he signs another person's name. Let an honest man enter the same bank, try to cash his own check, and he encounters some doubt. Why? Because the ordinary person wears more of his heart on his sleeve, for most of us a somewhat hesitant heart. The world senses this and responds hesitantly. The psychopath, however, is all confidence and ease, and the world is flimflammed.

Psychopathy is like those instances of tuberculosis that heighten the normal markings of the lungs and are almost invisible. Its diagnosis is easier in a hospital, where group reactions can be noted. It is important to be alert for a discrepancy between what the therapist feels about the patient and what most of the staff feels; the therapist will become the patient's lone defender, since only he may have received the full force of the patient's charm. This is "fossil diagnosis": people can be recognized by the imprints they leave behind. Similarly, depressed people depress the group, manic ones excite it—after a hysterical patient has left the conference, watch the men and women fight.

The chances of being duped are also lessened if one sets realistic expectations for human nature. The psychopathic mask of sanity is not a mask of ordinary sanity, which twitches and shows marks of strain. The accepted ideas of psychic health must be turned upside down—the person without any evidence of conflict, sadness, or regret is an exception and, in diagnostic work, suspect. He may have reached an unusual serenity, but he may just be unusually slick.

To the great delight of medical students and residents, these patients relate their histories back to the earliest years, replete with sexual details. Yet for all their wild adventures, psychopaths soon lose our interest. My patient unreeled his story with little indication of forgotten particulars. It seemed to be a movie he could project at will, but his detachment suggested that it was a movie about someone else. He glided through the academic, financial, and sexual troubles he had experienced since at least the age of eight, including the death of his mother, as if he wore a magic fairy-tale coat that protected him from any harm or influence. He exercised as little censorship over his memories as he did over his activities.

This ability in great people can give them the self-sufficiency to command vast armies or affairs of state. In the psychopathic person it is seen as a shallowness of affect, a light, aloof attitude that is comparable to the beautiful indifference of some hysterics. Indeed, so many are the similarities between hysteria and psychopathy—manipulativeness, seductiveness, theatricality— that each is sometimes claimed to be the female or male version of the other; both may run in the same family. This, if true, would be a sweet and overdue revenge on all those male physicians who have disparaged women as hysterics.

Psychiatry was first a consideration of symptoms and signs. The early scientific effort was to define and group them, as we are still doing, then to understand the mechanisms of their occurrence, and finally to track down the etiological agents, whether pathological relationships or pathological cells. One trail broadened into character and personality studies. Psychoanalysis described characteristic mechanisms or defensive organizations for the various personality types, such as a tendency to projection that may result in delusions and psychotic transferences. So too hospital psychiatrists concerned themselves with the premorbid disposition of symptomatic psychosis and delineated a number of types: schizoid, cyclothymic, paranoid. These seemed to merge with or lead to the familiar schizophrenic, manic, or paranoid psychoses. Jung's concept of the introvert and extrovert was another step in the same direction.

Thus a typology or personology arose, a nonsymptomatic psychiatry, quite impressionistic but increasingly capturing attention. The term *nonsymptomatic* is apt because the patients may not complain, although in our self-conscious age they sometimes bemoan their very characters. In another sense, however, the term *symptom* had only been extended. Personalities were soon regarded as symptomatic in themselves, enmeshed with previous experiences, special ways of solving conflict, or, in much European psychiatry, typical of a certain constitution or body type. There was a great effort to see the patient as a whole. Psychopathy came to roost among these personality or character disorders, inherent in the very ordering of the individual's way of life. But in this case the concept was never clear. Sometimes psychopathy meant little more than bad character. At all times it encompassed a vast range of capacities for behavioral control, from spontaneous violence to smooth, elaborate role playing. These patients seemed to have little more in common than a surface adaptability, a capacity to hide behind socially accepted forms.

Schizophrenic people are frozen in their fear; even the very paranoid are extraordinarily shy behind their defiant stares. Psychopaths, on the other hand, often appear cold, when not charming, because they do not seem to care, at least for us. Day-to-day schizophrenic life is sicklied over by reflection, fear, guilt, shame, and passivity. At first glance, my patient appeared to have cast all these away. I was the one who felt unsafe—but I knew he did not feel safe either. How could he, when I might turn on him in moral indignation? It has taken psychiatry a very long time to discover what a safe place for the psychopathic person might be like.

My patient had not completed many life tasks. He left home early. School, several jobs, and two engagements met the same fate. In another sense he had finished each task almost before starting it. He began, for example, one engagement to a rich and beautiful girl, presenting himself as a cousin to the Rockefellers with a complete family history, established wealth, and the best schooling. He did not dream these happy unrealities; he lived them. The portrayal of a handsome, rich scion vitalized the patient and he acted it naturally, cleverly putting off inquiries with a confident superiority and lightness. There were no unfinished parts to the life he played, the clothes he wore, the apartment he quickly furnished in which to entertain.

In one sense he was mad. His fantasies were destined to result in exposure and explosion, but he was not mad as people who hallucinate are mad, filling a desolate world from imagination and memory. My patient could create his imaginary world from reality, transiently changing the dancing figures of his imagination into the actual dancing figures of the golden life he loved. Hysterical people do the same, making us into father, mother, or brother to replay family dramas with real people who are only too glad to oblige. But psychopathy is distinguished by the extent to which reality is manipulated in these acts of immediate creation. "I should be rich, therefore I am rich." "He should be dead, then he dies." It is a Walter Mitty existence, not dreamt but realized.

Playacting is common to most people; having "the courage of one's convictions" means to adjust life to hope. Human striving is no more than the effort to cajole or forge reality into the shape of our dreams. What marks psychopathy is the rapidity with which the new reality is achieved, the methods used, the instability of the result, and above all the scarcity of inner change corresponding with the demands of the freshly created world. The rest of us, it is hoped, learn to expect less, work more, and change inside as much as we change the world outside.

From an early age, first in the military school his father hoped would straighten him out, later in his social circles, my patient would join a group of boys, then men, who were fiercely attracted to each other, constantly shifting their allegiances, and intensely jealous. Potential members knew each other at a glance and exchanged the rousing passwords of a secret society against the world. The male body was king, just as the female body rules the magazine covers of conventional life. The patient passed through these companionships as he did every other, making no final commitments, concealing the envy he felt, and managing rather than entering relationships. Young women frightened and disgusted him, older women were to be exploited. He felt drawn to free, careless, bold boys who thrust against life without reserve.

Many psychopathic people have brief psychoses when blocked from action. My patient did not experience such periods of acute confusion and delusion. But he did have many bouts of depression, feeling sad, empty, and tired. This was not the kind of depression in which he berated himself or felt pangs of conscience—rather, he was downcast and felt mistreated. During these intervals, which occurred when he was not involved in playing a role, the desire for young men was overriding. He wanted to look at the exciting ones, lie next to them, and orally enjoy the admired parts. The relationships were brief but satisfying, and he felt secure in having access to such medicine for his ennui.

The patient had one other cure besides playacting and the contacts with boys (almost like a swallowing of them). He swallowed amphetamines obtained with prescriptions that he wrote himself. These pills, unlike the newer antidepressants, reproduced the firmness and vitality of the other two experiences. He had learned how to use amphetamines wisely, taking a little, elevating the dose slowly, and then abstaining for several days as his tolerance subsided. He moved from one to another of the three solutions, acting, using boys, and taking drugs, all of them actions of which society disapproves, to control his unbearable emotions. Note that the cures are his own treatment, as tubercles are the response of the body to bacilli.

The three actions indicate a mechanism at work in psychopathy, a principle that connects the relief of sadness to acting, eating, and taking drugs. Sadness suggests a missing element, and the others suggest something added: a new part in life, a new person, a new inner state. With the first my patient rejoined society in a fresh identity; the second joined a new person to him; and with the third he briefly transformed himself from within.

Despite the patient's appearance of self-sufficiency, his insufficiency now becomes obvious. He had to have special things to eat. He could not be alone. He could not control himself; society had to do that for him. He could not be himself: now and then my patient would look around masterfully and wink, not to anyone in particular but because he had admired the gesture in another man. Should a wild hope evaporate, his heart sank, despair mounted, and he would reject the fairest prize to show the world its burning injustice—all of this camouflaged by a confident smile.

In conjunction with this painful incompleteness was an entitlement to flout rules and exploit other people. Although the patient appeared to be self-centered, he needed others to establish, control, and feed him, to mimic and identify with. Yet much that was other had its only significance in terms of himself. He gathered the external world around him like a cloak that was tailored to his purposes alone, used, constantly searched for any rips or defects, thrown aside.

Incompleteness and entitlement are often related. The lack of inner ideals and identity may free psychopathic people to act as they will. Also, the lack of ideals and identity may spring from early life experiences producing the feelings of injustice that further entitle them to act.

* * *

Nowhere in psychiatry is the evidence of a relationship between early experience and symptoms so firm as in psychopathy. All the evidence is circumstantial; psychopathic monkeys have not been produced, if they would be recognizable, as catatonic ones have. Nevertheless, circumstantial evidence can be strong: when you discover, in Thoreau's words, a trout in the milk.

It has been shown that some psychopathic acts are repetitions of experiences that the patient had in childhood, not as aggressor but as victim; the arsonist has sometimes been badly burned as a child. Psychopathy occurs with more frequency when one parent is absent and the other is extraordinarily inconsistent in discipline, and when children grow up in large institutions without parental figures. (In these same circumstances the incidence of neurosis appears to fall below the average.) Finally there is evidence, more difficult to establish in statistical terms, that parents whose own prohibitions are weak and inconsistent may bequeath these deficiencies to their children. Folk wisdom has attested to this for many centuries, but perhaps we can retrieve for science, medicine, and practical action what were intuitions or common sense.

My patient's father ostensibly disapproved of his son's behavior. Yet a strange thing happened when he spoke of the boy's shams and thefts: he became animated and knew about his son's actions in extraordinary detail; at least twice he dreamed of doing similar things himself. He said he had also been embittered by the mother's death and resented the staid, spinster aunts and their wealth. He was not the easy charmer his son was; this solid, correct man could not reproduce the son's hypnotic smile. But when talking of the boy's conduct, he was like his twin. Parents are expected to have aspirations for their children and even burden them with desires for what the parents missed. Suppose the parents long to steal or are secret enemies of their relatives and friends?

August Aichhorn was the student of psychopathy whose contributions to treatment seem deepest and longest in reach. Director of a school for delinquent boys, he did something unexpected when his charges did the least unexpected thing imaginable. They stole from him, sometimes his belongings, sometimes his language and mannerisms. The unexpected thing he did was to welcome the theft: if imitation is the sincerest form of flattery, burglary, he thought, cannot be far behind. Perhaps these boys are "needy," taking something they need. Perhaps too they feel entitled to take these things because what they need is what everyone needs and, from a human point of view, what everyone is entitled to have. They just happen to be without. His was an act of generosity almost without parallel. What is it that they need? The answer was partly Aichhorn, this admirable director of the school. He offered himself.

Now the outlines of the psychopathic safe place are emerging. The makers of this place must feel safe in being idealized and stolen from. They must also be able to identify with those who steal from them. While setting the necessary limits for continuance of the community, they must remain close enough to its members to permit the crucial identifications. Such communities have often had a religious base. They have also been, as with Alcoholics Anonymous, communities of brethren, of equals, of like afflicted, because there acceptance and the safety of being with one's own are more likely to occur. And the deeply spiritual dimension of AA encourages the necessary idealization and internalization that spring not only from a society of mutual admiration but from a higher power and a greater ideal to which all can aspire.

Another result of Aichhorn's experience was to recast our very ideas of sickness and health. Stealing might not be sick or bad: it might be a reaching for health. The revolution in perception of psychological life that Freud set in motion was here carried a step further, into the territory of values, ideals, the very means by which we constitute our selves. I cannot just be myself or know myself. However long I look into the mirror, I see only the self constituted by a misleading, stable, concrete image. In fact, I cannot constitute myself. I actually find myself outside myself, as those sad, delinquent boys learned.

So hungry for an identity that they would take in and spit out innumerable mimicked existences, they found livable and solid fare at Aichhorn's place. It was livable because the ideals he represented were constructive: it could become a lasting part of the boys because it was not just imitated, its appearances not simply worn. Aichhorn's closeness and his love for them formed connecting points through which a real absorption could occur. At one time the patients had become whatever they wanted; now they wanted someone they could really become. Once the delinquents stood apart and played parts; now they could make Aichhorn a part of themselves. Henceforth it would not be easy to play roles because their new stable identity would expose them.

My patient shifted from one dazzled, frightened, or angry mirror to another, working his way onto these ephemeral spaces and then suddenly away again. The difficulty was not that he lived off others; to a considerable extent everyone needs to do that. In part the difficulty was that he could not become whatever was needed to please others more than transiently; he only pretended. At first glance this suggests the old theme of fooling and being fooled, of seduction and betrayal. But that's not the theme either. For one thing, society resounds daily with events of fooling and being fooled, often to the advantage of the deceiver. My patient suffered in a way that was both more poignant and less forgiven.

This is illustrated by a series of events that shook two hospitals and made some of us shake in our shoes. I had just been put in charge of several in-patient psychiatric services. My chief was a wonderfully wise man whose capacity for surprise seemed to have been exhausted years earlier. We admitted to one of these services a boy of eighteen, Mediterranean in looks and style, dark and full of romance. Six years before, Benito had set fire to a building, or so he was charged, in which two old people died. The intervening period was spent in a series of school-hospitals that he had now outgrown. Lacking August Aichhorn and a genuinely remedial environment, he was sent to us, perhaps the most serious of all the deceptions and self-deceptions with which the case abounded.

If God has a sense of humor or Nature a capacity to enjoy irony, the universe must have rocked with laughter at the environment into which the young man was dropped. We were proud to be an ''open hospital'': patients came and went between the various services and facilities and, often, the outside world. The environment that Benito entered was aboundingly medical. There were several hospitals in the area, each with a full complement of operating rooms—which turned out to be of great interest to Benito. Psychopathic and hysterical patients often have *idées fixes*, fantasies that are somewhere between daydream and delusion: not firmly believed and not easily forgotten. Benito half-believed he was a surgeon. But he was not so out of touch with reality that he did not need the accoutrements of surgery, operating rooms, patients, other surgeons, to embody the idea. Here we, and surgery itself, wonderfully cooperated. Our doors were open, the hospitals were nearby, and even the doors of the operating rooms were accessible because, don mask and gown and confidence, no one knows who you are in a bustling medical complex. So it was not long before Benito was attending an alarming number of the operations in the city, usually standing by, occasionally holding a retractor, always, so far as I could learn, the perfect guest. There he was, dreaming his wonderful dream and, best of all, living it in the busy, serious, useful company of surgical work. All this we discovered later.

Gradually he concentrated his efforts on one hospital and one operating room. Benito did not want to be any surgeon; he dreamed of being the greatest one in the world. The operating room he chose was the place of work of a famous heart surgeon, whose remarkable accomplishments were the stuff of headlines and interviews around the globe. Benito pretended to be a visiting medical student, and it was not long before he was a familiar, accepted part of the group. Caps, masks, and gowns could be discarded in the comradely locker-room atmosphere after surgery. The great man was fond of Benito and wrote him an encouraging letter of recommendation.

Now we approach the ''difficulty'' that is not simply a matter of needing others or being deceptive. Benito began to wonder where the surgeon lived, found out his address, and one evening visited his home. Later he told me he had often gone there, circling the large house with its tall shrubbery and lighted windows, gradually growing bolder until he would press his face against those windows, all but push himself through, to be part of that family, to be part of the great man himself. It made me want to cry to feel such yearning in this boy who never had a home of his own, who now saw it so close.

The ending is familiar. Benito was caught at the window, his record of arson discovered, and the heat was turned on us. I remember being in my chief's office when the angry surgeon called. We were ready: we knew about the letter of recommendation, the visits to the house, the family's sensible terror. My chief listened patiently, holding the phone away from his ear in self protection, and the anger subsided. It seems a long time ago now—the chief and the surgeon are both dead—but I can almost hear the old psychiatrist's quiet voice asking how the surgeon met the boy, eliciting a startled memory of the letter of recommendation, honoring his willingness to acknowledge it, closing gently without apology or condemnation: "Sometimes a little friendship goes a long way."

Here is the difficulty I mentioned. Benito did not merely need or deceive. His hunger was so deep that he could take a gesture of friendship for a promise of love; and he could have taken a failure of that love for a warrant to set fire. Society has long known the last danger, but still does not accept what lies behind it. The pathogenic sequence that appears to start with family deprivation leads to seductions that make us all part of the sequence, and potentially part of its treatment.

The same point is made by the very tone of this chapter. Surely my description of these two patients suffers from the quality with which I have charged them, a certain superficiality or distance that allows the inner person to escape. The reader may have wondered how safe I felt, seeing that I had to hold back from these charming and dangerous people. In this section on the most difficult situations, psychopathy transcends even suicide and psychosis in the problems it creates.

Such are the demands of safe-place making, so different from the first response produced in us by others. We have to learn how to be still when the other needs to be left alone but asks for intervention, to give confidence when the patient induces despair, to find strength when everything suggests madness and deviance, to bring sobriety to those who would set us afire, and the largest demand of all: sometimes to *be* what the patient needs, both embodying an ideal and guiding that ideal toward a life to be lived.

Today
and
Tomorrow

CHAPTER 9

SULLIVAN AND THE HEART

Recently a middle-aged man appeared at the admissions office of a university hospital and asked to donate his heart. He said he wanted to give it to a dying patient. I don't know what happened, but one can imagine the consternation this must have caused among nurses, heart surgeons, and, later, the psychiatrists and ethicists who might be called in. The surgeons would be of two minds: this was a heaven-sent opportunity and yet they had little in the way of proven contrivances with which to replace the proffered organ. No doubt the psychiatrists were supposed to decide if the man was suicidal or mad; the profession's diagnostic uncertainties would soon become apparent. I suspect the ethicists would be the most perplexed: for one thing, how would they respond if the generous man protested the immorality of removing hearts from nonconsenting baboons while refusing his voluntary gift?

This scene from the birth of a new society is my starting point for a discussion of a dynamic social psychiatry for our time. How would Harry Stack Sullivan, dead now some forty years, have set about diagnosing the would-be heart donor? How would he have dealt with the powerful conventions and prejudices converging on such a clinical field? And what help would this great student of the interpersonal be able to offer in finding, and giving, some measure of freedom and self-respect amid the powers and agencies posited by our deterministic, developmental theories?

It is hardly noteworthy that any institution, whether hospital, medicine, or the system of social values, has difficulty responding rationally to free, novel acts. The partly internalized system of public pressures by which average behavior is shaped, by which human independence is both protected and subverted, works best when the traditional and the individual converge on occasions that we can call consensual. An example is when I can both give my heart and keep it, as might be said of matrimony. The point is that in some ceremonies not too many questions are asked; and even if protestors are requested, they are told to forever hold their peace. This is one reason Sullivan has never been a very popular establishment figure: he asked too many questions.

The occasion about which Sullivan asked the most embarrassing questions was the psychiatric interview, a central topic of all these chapters. Or putting the same point in academic style, he was our foremost clinical epistemologist. He was not only skeptical of the value of everyday history taking, as Freud was; he went a step further to the relativism and scientific instrumentalism that are so commonplace today. There can be no one-person observations; psychological observation is a function of the field or context or method that is part of the observation. Therefore, if we set out to imagine what Sullivan would tell us now, the most obvious answer would be: I told you so. My example of the man trying to give away his heart shows this in a fresh perspective.

How would Sullivan have decided whether the would-be heart

donor was a publicity hound trying to get on talk shows, an impostor-Munchausen case seeking closeness to doctors and perhaps mutilative surgery, an isolated miserable individual fed up with life, or a sweet self-sacrificing soul doing the right thing? Here again Sullivan could say "I told you so," since his three categories of the ambition-ridden, the asocial, and the inadequate have resemblances to the cases just mentioned. The ambitious and impostors invade the field, shaping it to their own purposes; depressives draw us into their self-depreciation; and the inadequate are often empty vessels waiting to be filled. In short, the interpersonal means the characterological, and often in subtler and more practical ways than those provided by the contemporary distinctions of "borderline" and "narcissistic." Also Sullivan, faithful to his teacher William Alanson White, looked for what the patient was trying to do. He would have kept open the possibility that the heart donor's intention was none of the above, but something unexpected, even unique.

Still further, Sullivan would have been more interested than we are in the ways by which those nurses, surgeons, psychiatrists, and ethicists shape the processes of diagnosis and treatment, and are shaped by them. I don't mean only their prejudices and expectations, each group's baggage of received truth; I mean especially the ways by which each group enters actively the business of world-making, as it has come to be called.

Nurses and doctors are quite naturally sensitive to how patients' behavior endangers their health. This professional concentration on physical hygiene can create an aseptic world remarkably free of much that is pleasurable or adventuresome. Churchill, on being told he would live twenty years longer if he did not drink, smoke, or eat so much, is reported to have said, "It would only *seem* twenty years longer." The transformation of health values into pervasive moral values can be compared, in its psychic and social effects, with the processes that the Baron von Uexküll described in his theoretical biology. Each animal's world, he indicated, is shaped by its sensory apparatus: the caterpillar, which contacts the world chiefly through chemoreceptors, inhabits a world largely of smells or tastes. This becomes increasingly evident to humans as scientific devices bring in data hitherto unimaginable and show us a world vastly different from that of our five senses. The same process is at work in the psychological and social sphere. Our values shape a world that excludes some kinds of behavior or throws them into a penumbra of the forbidden or evil. I have noticed, for example, that the medical clinging to physical health and life, often at the expense of everything else, makes poor companions of medicine and psychiatry. Not only is the quality of life likely to be sacrificed to its mere prolongation, but behavior that appears suicidal meets the joint indignation of medicine and church. I am not recommending suicide. But I do maintain that behavior one wants to deal with therapeutically is best not met with indignation or fury. This is a problem for many medical institutions I have known. It could also be a problem for the heart donor. Would the medical community honor a value transcending personal health?

I believe Sullivan would have been especially delighted with the ethicists. "I surmise," we can hear him saying, "that they are interested in life principally as it is affected by death. Putting aside speculations about thanatos or the closely related and much discussed hostile introjects, the ethicists' interest in death comes down to the rights of murder and suicide. Here we can expect society to have much to say. As generally responsible spokesmen in eminently respectable institutions, the ethicists will provide many ingenious arguments to rid us of people either notably unattractive or very expensive." This is how the baboon problem occurs. Murdering our near ancestors for the purposes of scientific development, more specifically to save our own skins, troubles only a fringe of people eccentric and sentimental. It is also widely accepted that sacrificing one's life, as in war, is justified, especially if you manage to take a few of the enemy with you. What the heart donor conflates is this whole set of divergent values. Is it all right to sacrifice oneself in the war against heart disease? Do such wars have to be officially declared by Congress? More directly, does the individual have the right to enter into final actions with mass blessing? In part it is the old problem of society and solitude that Sullivan pondered so long.

He emerged with a quite different view from that of his existential colleague Erich Fromm. For Sullivan society was the ground of both hope and disease but somehow preferable to solitude, of which he had perhaps experienced too much. In contrast, for Fromm society was an occasion for escape, with some measure of solitude the condition of freedom and independence. I think it is important in this calculus that Fromm was the more comfortably sociable of the two, and so perhaps more tempted to sell out. Most likely Sullivan's independence could survive any social encounter, even be accentuated by it. It is still further illuminating that Freud's attitude appears to differ from either: his is an example of extraordinary world-making. That boundless spirit needed the world in order to find his independence; he needed the world to make his mark, like Caesar or Napoleon. As a result, there was no danger of his being subverted by society or isolated from it. In Freud, society had almost met its match.

We would therefore not expect Freud to be much interested in individual rights. As with Schopenhauer and Nietzsche, the important thing was strength of will or instincts. For this reason, I believe, both Sullivan and Fromm speak to the ordinary man in more realistic language than Freud does. I myself can be subverted by society; my need for society is great—I am very far from Freud's self-image of a great rock against which the waves of history batter and are spent. My conclusion is that Sullivan would have seen the heart donor as needing considerable support against the forces of established conviction: it would do no good to assume a neutral, anonymous, silent posture of waiting for reason to prevail. However mysterious in the Freudian system is the transmutation of instinct into reason, it was Freud's great hope, perhaps because his own reason was, like an instinct, of such extraordinary power. In different words, we can say that Sullivan's concept of treatment was closer to advocacy than Freud's was.

Treatment as advocacy means protection against the world, including that part of the world represented by the therapist. As we set about imagining how Sullivan would have diagnosed and treated the heart donor, the idea of advocacy will never be far away. Indeed I read Sullivan as being close enough to the existential point of view to see diagnosis as itself in need of treatment, that is, treatment of an exclusively diagnostic stance. Further, Sullivan believed that diagnosis is never a matter of simply uncovering or recognizing a condition: it is also a creating of conditions together by patient and doctor. So it becomes of central importance not to create a condition that is itself irremediable.

The ambitious (we can include here an impostor version of the heart donor) represented for Sullivan the most difficult group of all therapeutic problems. I don't know that he found them quite so difficult diagnostically, perhaps because he had an ear for phoniness that surpasses most. I expect that the only body of therapists today widely experienced with the ambitious are the training analysts of psychoanalytic institutes. Because institute graduation is now a professional and social cachet (it was once the opposite), what someone has called a means of upward social mobility, a training analysis must be partly a treatment of ambition. The situation is not improved when the treatment of the ambitious is so often conducted by the ambitious. Kohut has addressed the problem from an existential perspective. Here is the interpersonal one, from Sullivan:

The ambition-ridden person comes to the psychiatrist to get what he can in the way of aid in his career. He may be willing to pay for this. He may be most determined in his efforts to achieve it. But he lives in a world of competitive violence and necessary compromise, and he will have none of the psychiatrist's skepticism about the finality of this formula. He cannot escape the competitive attitude, even in this regard, and all too frequently by dint of competing with the physician at every step, reduces the potentially therapeutic situation to a struggle about who is doctor and who is patient. If the psychiatrist remains detached in his attitude towards the incessant demands for recognition, the patient's insecurity is apt to disrupt the situation. The problem is chiefly one of following a course between a fraudulent acceptance of the juvenile motivation as satisfactory . . . and an emphatic insistence that even the patient's most satisfactory interpersonal relations are inadequate. Given the necessary interest, and tact and patience, one may come gradually to progress with one of these patients to a more mature relationship . . . The long preliminaries are often interrupted before this achievement, often, I surmise, for the convenience of the physician.

It is not likely that the heart-donor impostor, seeking to get on talk shows, would find himself in treatment; yet this negative expectation itself shows the close ties between diagnosis and treatment. What sort of hospitality could a patient so diagnosed get from us? Surely much of the same contempt that the impostor himself often dispenses. And I have encountered people ambitious even to the point of fraudulence whom I came to see quite differently: ambition was not the problem. One such patient I treated was busy deceiving three women simultaneously, plus a wealthy patron. What emerged was the intractability of his situation. As a boy he had been shunted between two not very satisfactory family situations, as a kind of orphan-prince. He married, largely at the woman's pregnant insistence, and then was drawn into a circle of two more exciting women. Little of this could be divulged to his puritanical patron. My point is that his healthy side proved to be the opposite of what it first seemed. I came to believe that the difficulty was his passive acceptance of marriage—really the respectable thing he did— and that his apparent psychopathy was a further expression of this passivity. Naturally it was a point he found refreshing. It was also one that he could not act on for a long time. That required more of the courage with which he had at first seemed too well supplied.

Nowadays, I suspect, our heart donor would be found suicidal and depressed; he might have a "major affective disorder." This is so much the rage that any schizophrenic would be wise to take on a bit of affective coloring to avoid still further neglect. Not that fashions in diagnosis are anything new. In the 1920s diagnoses of underlying homosexuality were the rage (try that today); in the 1950s almost every patient was either hysterical or schizophrenic; now it is mania and affective disorders. One reason for this psychiatric faddishness was Sullivan's central concern: he knew how difficult it is to achieve reliable psychological observations. There are interviewers who can make almost anyone seem psychotic. The distorting lenses of our everyday clinical habits can turn ordinary people into monsters—no great psychiatric trick. I recall clinical presentations as a resident, aimed at uncovering, emphasizing, above all never overlooking any piece of possible psychopathology, which appeared strange when set beside the interview of a fairly ordinary human being by a fairly empathic observer. I have already remarked that the absence of yardsticks, the power of interactive effects, and our preoccupation with psychopathology while we lack tests and standards of normality make securing reliable observations, much less diagnoses, extraordinarily difficult. And the current fashion is to think that the whole task can be accomplished in a single examination, by questions and answers, on the basis of research protocols.

Just as we are adept at making diseases appear, so can we make them vanish. Recently a group from one of the foremost centers for the biological and descriptive study of schizophrenia announced that the disease schizophrenia cannot be found; it may not even exist. Apparently schizophrenia does not pass the tests for being a disease on grounds of description, epidemiology, course, or treatment; even the much touted genetic studies, many from the same institution, are not all that compelling. This would have been a source of vast amusement to Sullivan.

Perhaps we can again summon up his voice: "The good news goes forth. We are at last free of schizophrenia. Having banished it from the state hospitals, we can now banish it from our thoughts. The patients will be able to look on this with special irony. Having known social banishment most of their lives, they can now learn that this was all illusion. They are, in fact, nowhere to be found." You may not be surprised to learn that the scientific banishers of schizophrenia are still able to embrace the affective disorders. Perhaps the heart donor is sufficiently depressed and suicidal to require shock treatment—in which case an arrythmia is precipitated, and a small myocardial infarction. The problem is solved: his heart is no longer desirable.

As a rule, the diagnosis of inadequate personality is a last resort. Not clearly psychotic yet much battered by life, these patients drift about the wards as inadequately understood as they are "inadequate." From considerable experience both on state hospital wards and in my private practice, I conclude that many are among the nicest people to be found. They can be long-suffering to saintly extents; sometimes they have empathic resources beyond the reach of most of us; they take on the coloring, though faintly, of those around them and appear before us because their goodness is hazardous. I like to quote the Russian proverb, ''Be a lamb and the wolf will appear.'' The predatory abound among us, indeed probably inhabit all of us. The dear but unprotected often appear inadequate; God knows they are adequate enough prey. Worse, this has often been the story of their lives, so that whatever opportunities they had for soul or self building were snatched from them. Surprisingly, some of the inadequate prove to have been quite adequate earlier in life, having fallen apart only under the heaviest pressures. Critical to the development of these once-adequates, in my experience, are early and intense identifications with authoritarian figures seemingly of the highest ideals: in one case, the lordly matron of an orphanage. This identification did not result in the patient's herself becoming lordly, but in a pursuit of the same high ideals as a servant. This made her the instant slave of any imperious person, and she seemed capable of bringing out imperiousness in individuals otherwise pretty docile. I call this the Munich phenomenon, after what Hitler did to the British and French: the good and hopeful brought out the worst in human nature. The patient thought very poorly of herself, dressed and carried herself accordingly, and was regarded as an eccentrically weak and deferential creature, even if exceedingly busy. Treatment got nowhere until she found someone who could both resist pushing her around and provide some protection against her oppressors.

It is possible that the heart donor was cut from the same cloth. That is, he may have been following some inner or outer command to be good and lethally self-sacrificing, after he realized that his own life was not worth living. I always feel Sullivan's sympathy for the underdog, especially in contrast to the hysterical top dogs. He is the least likely of psychiatrists to blame the underdog for being that; he is the least likely to see the underdog as masochistic or otherwise designing his own humiliations. This is not to say that both parties do not share some responsibility for most transactions. The point is that the two parties may differ in their powers. The world's experience with Hitler and Stalin—men of enormous will—should have made this clear, though it has not. As Freud wrote, the economic factor is of all our categories the most neglected, and this pertains to the economics of power. It is important to emphasize how powerful some wills are and how much assistance most of us need in order to resist them. Someone has remarked that goodness may be far more destructive than evil because it is not constrained by conscience. This is the death knell of the inadequate. Many, devoted to the good, become prisoners of those with apparently noble motives. It can begin in childhood when parents add high ideals to the authority of parenthood.

Surely no problem has more interested the best minds of our nation than this issue of individual freedom and power in relation to society and competing centers of interest. It preoccupied to an extraordinarily productive extent the Founding Fathers, producing a concept, not theirs alone, of the balance of powers in the framing of this country's constitution. It greatly concerned Ralph Waldo Emerson, who spoke ringingly for each man's obligation to be himself, against the forces of custom and conformity. It concerned William James, as he struggled toward a pluralistic universe in which truth was to be the judgment of actions and not the Hegelian overarching One. Sullivan belongs to this American tradition: specifically, his bringing down to the level of individual and social perception the fogs of preconception and misunderstanding that therapy was meant to pierce. The challenge is no less today. The psychiatry and psychoanalysis we inherit, so much of it a European hierarchical system in origin, asks us to accept developmental and epigenetic speculations before which the individual is supposed to be helpless, even grateful—all in the name of truth and health.

We came through a national time, in the 1960s, when traditions and institutions were questioned and found wanting, with a force not experienced since the Revolution and Civil War. An American president was deposed in part by means of secret recording devices that may remind us of how Sullivan first studied another secret place, the interview. Today there are currents reminiscent of the complacent 1950s—yet little is the same. And in psychiatry we are in part back where we started at the turn of the century, searching for diseases and biological processes. Yet here too it is not the same. Today there are many more competing forces in our pluralistic society and in the profession of psychiatry, often overlapping society and profession, as with the women's movement, minority protest, gay rights, adoptees' rights, and the very rapidly changing climate of sexuality.

The fact remains that we "bring up" children and are expected to impart values. Even God no longer seems so dead. We must still ask: how is one generation's wisdom to be passed on without tyranny? How can freedom and authority, independence and institutions, coexist? How can ideals, including religious ideals, coexist with a community of independence and questioning? The modern period is marked by frequent public complaints that parents have abdicated their responsibilities, have not transmitted values. But this abdication was frequently purposeful, in the interest of children's freedom to find their own ideals.

I believe that a fresh solution to this problem lies in an area still much fought over and accessible to little more than intuition and clinical impressions. Perhaps D. W. Winnicott was the student of the problem whose intuitions remain the most impressive. He saw independent selfhood as being born in the experience of one's own impulses, with the amplification and acknowledgment of those impulses by the original caring figures. Selfhood, he suggested, arises in the first experienced society, but it must be a society able to respect the child's solitude, letting the child alone. To my knowledge Winnicott did not extend this line of thought to the relation between self and authority. He did not tell us how values are transmitted without the destruction of self. By giving such importance to the concept of self, however, both Winnicott and Sullivan point to where I believe the solution lies.

I will approach it by telling another heart story, also of recent occurrence and perhaps still more psychologically wrenching than the first. Newspapers reported the following: an adolescent boy fell in love with a girl of the same age; she rejected him; he continued to pine after her and told his family of unfamiliar head pains; the girl was known to have an inoperable congenital heart lesion; the boy died, seemingly of a brain aneurysm, and prior to his death made arrangements to have his heart given to her; this was done. Subsequently the girl is reported to have said that she had not known how much he loved her. Doubtless no one has ever given a heart so literally and completely before. This must be cheering to those who fear the death of feeling in our technological time.

Let us try to imagine the girl's experience. Pretend that she came to one of us for treatment of guilt and a pain in her heart. Imagine that she felt the heart was not hers nor was she worthy of it, and at the same time she knew she couldn't live without it. She might hesitantly say that the boy had been cruel, literally stealing into her heart when she didn't want him: he had conquered her after all. Here is the connection to what I have been saying about transmitting values to children who are sometimes not at home with them. Both the heart donor and many parents have made their loved ones obligated, even imprisoned. Neither the heart recipient nor many children are free. But how is freedom given? More specifically, if it is even possible for such a thing as freedom to be *given*, how can it be done in a family or therapeutic setting where so many other forces are at work?

The pieces of our picture puzzle lie scattered about, in different sizes and colors, with only the hint of a figure here or a vista there. Yet if two or three can be fitted together, the overall design will begin to emerge. Still, a puzzle reveals its full meaning only when completed, because each piece makes a contribution to the whole.

I started out with an example of free, novel decision making that does not fit easily into the established system of public pressures. I suggested that the heart donor might find at least a temporary place if he were a publicity seeker looking for talk shows. This is a curious feature of impostors. Some have told me they felt deeply alone and alienated; yet they were able at least for a while to fit in wonderfully. That only sharpens the contrast between society and solitude. The impostor patient of the Munchausen type makes a still more valiant and destructive effort to fit in, often plays the role of both doctor and patient, creating, sometimes by extravagant self-treatment, an illness that will find a place in the medical system, even to the point of mutilative surgery. The values here are medicine, doctoring, being a patient; the narrow but extraordinary freedom is to create in the complex system of healing a particular, jagged, trumped-up piece that as soon as it is discovered is thrown away. I don't know any more pathetic effort in the whole tapestry of individuals' relationships to society.

Depression and suicidality snap neatly into the psychiatric system, because large parts of the system's practices, alertness, medications, electrical interventions, locked hospitals, and laws of commitment are designed for just those exigencies. But what fits into psychiatry does not fit into life, indeed offends convention when it cannot escape from it once and for all. The rights to speak, assemble, and vote have not been joined by the right to die. In a century in which the right to kill has been exercised with unprecedented efficiency, frequency, and sometimes honor, the right to die still stands outcast because, as I have suggested, it is an individual and not a mass decision. It comes closer to respectability when it approaches a public decision, as now appears to be the case with patients on kidney dialysis (many of whom make a decision to die) or as may soon be the case with AIDS patients. Note this seemingly necessary piece of our picture puzzle, the transformation of the individual into the consensual, even conventional.

The transformation is a small part of what I referred to as world-making. Its obverse is the inadequate. Here a world is imposed, not made. Much of what I have been saying comes down to the question of values versus freedom: can a world be made that is not imposed? The puzzle metaphor works here too. Everyone recognizes the pleasant feeling of finding one large piece into which several others fit. What we are searching for, however, is something different. Like the puzzle solver trying a piece in many places, let us try a piece shaped something like this: how is the individual to find his own convention, make his own world, without needing to have the force and reason of a Freud?

It is time to look again at a different part of the puzzle, the epistemological part so close to Sullivan's heart. Not only is psychological knowledge difficult of access; in the clinical setting it is, as I have suggested, demonstrably approximate and to some measure uncertain. This uncertainty at first surprises and then should delight us. It is almost the final piece in the picture of the clinical relationship of the individual and society, in particular of freedom and values.

Let me ask again, why is psychological knowledge approximate? Because it is always at least partly historical: as soon as we have established that something seems true about the patient, we have transformed the truth. We have made it into something that is looked at, interpreted, above all something that may be challenged or corrected. This is why insights are so fragile. Everyone knows how they can be sought after, seized on, lived happily with for a while, and then found wanting. Sometimes a dream brings us an image that seems to go to the heart of our wishes or the human condition. That image is also an insight, and like other insights it points both backward and forward, to what seems to have been true but what might be transcended. It stands, we can say, between reality and the ideal. The past streams into the present, and so does the future. This explains the extraordinary vulnerability of present psychological truth: it is constantly subject to review and attack by both past and future.

Why is psychological knowledge historical in a way that chemical and physical knowledge is not? The reason is that psychology takes as its material the subjective, the way we see things; it attempts to be objective about the subjective. If I tell you that rubies are green, this statement becomes of psychological interest, rather than of chemical or optic interest, when you learn it occurred to me while falling asleep, in a particular state of mind. These states of mind constitute subjectivity, acts of seeing, thinking, dreaming, feeling. In order to be objective about the subjective, psychology has to confront the fact that it studies itself, it studies itself studying itself, ad infinitum. This is not simply a repeatable experiment with a fixed outcome, since each act of studying transforms at least a little the very subjectivity being studied. We can say that learning occurs.

Many would like to eliminate the subjective, or at least reduce it all to error, dream, and madness: the subjective is to be replaced by the objective. The reason this effort is doomed reveals itself most chillingly when it is most nearly successful, when we encounter a subjectivity transformed by the worship of objectivity into something cold, indifferent, even monstrous (see many modern hospitals). Then we meet not the disappearance of subjectivity but its reappearance as a certain view of science and humanity—for example, I don't care about your feelings and your particularity, only about your body.

Psychotherapy is the name we give efforts to study and improve one's experience and view of things—one's subjectivity—with the help of another's subjectivity. We want to be as objective as possible about others, but we have to recognize that psychotherapy is shot through with the subjective and the historical. When we work with a patient for an understanding of a life, uncertainty is everywhere—the context of the search, the unknown past, the future streaming in—and yet both patient and therapist would like to know, to settle. Surprisingly often both can, but let them beware: settlements are uncertain and, still more important, both may be capable of creating a better future that defies what seemed so certain. In this way, process becomes more important than explanation, while explanation is continually enlarged by process.

The systematic uncertainty of psychological knowledge, its being always in process, like the cutting edge of science generally, has its analogue in individual development. Lawrence Kohlberg hypothesized a course of moral development that leads from impulse to fixed superego to the emergence and selection of ideals of one's own. In Winnicott's language, just as impulse is experienced, acknowledged, and then owned as one's own, so values have to be discovered, reflected on, and then selected as one's own. I have already discussed Freud's similar formula: the ego ideal is the inheritor of primitive narcissism. Independence is to be exercised in discovering what is authoritative for oneself, and in continuing to reflect upon it.

Could the girl make peace with the transplanted heart? Or would it always be a foreign body tearing her apart? Is there a psychotherapist, confronting a patient's internal objects and her external relationships, who has not asked the same question? And what of our first heart donor, perhaps the pioneer of a new charity, a new way of giving made possible by new technology— how is it to be decided whether the gift is value or madness, life or death? Surely this is only one more example of a self-reflective process carried up into social reflection, exemplified by contemporary discussions of sexual values and the relation between the sexes and between groups generally, dominators and dominated, perhaps most notably between children and adults. Here again Sullivan would have been at home, ready to hear in the child's voice what the adult had forgotten or thrust aside, trying to clear the social field of prejudice, projection, the dominance of position and pride, hoping to hear in the adult what fear and submission had thrust aside.

What I suggest is this. The search for clinical conditions within which reliable observations can be made points in two directions: toward the need to deflect the preconceptions and projections dominating clinical fields and toward an attitude going beyond respect for the patient, substituting instead a real democracy of relationship between therapist and patient. The old hierarchies are to be dismantled. These conditions of reliable inquiry are also, I suggest, necessary for a viable relationship between freedom and structure, between individual determination and the passing on of values. Sullivan did not hesitate to advise patients, even to direct and, some would say, manipulate them. But his activity was in the service of clearing the field, of counteracting the forces of pride and prejudice that cloud perception; we can say it was countermanipulative. And the field was being cleared so that patients could decide for themselves.

There is a close parallel to this structured freedom giving in the work of Winnicott. You recall that the supportive mother was to create a safe space around her child in which the child could find and be itself. Something similar has to be provided for those many patients who never had this self-building relationship with their parents. Here the parallel to Sullivan's participant observation is most obvious. In clearing the field, Sullivan's interactions give back to the patient Winnicott's free space. Neither party is allowed to invade or dominate the other.

It is a short step, I believe, to the final piece in our picture puzzle. Authority is seemingly the implacable invader of personal freedom in the name of society's need for conformity. Is personality inevitably compromised, as psychoanalytic theory so often suggests? The way out that Winnicott implied cannot go this far. The mother who can amplify the child's wishes and not impose her own has to be a rare creature. But rarer still must be that human situation in which the child can grow up free of conflict with its surroundings. For my part, Freud was right: conflict is inevitable. The child must be imposed on. The way to self-possession, in other words, does not arrive in the form of a society compatible with the individual's wishes. Such an idea transcends the expectations of even the most utopian vision.

The way to self-possession comes about in the acceptance of impulses and values as one's own, those of one's self. Of course there must be compromise, with the constant danger of selling out. But even the extreme case of a young girl with a heart not her own, the heart of someone she had refused, illustrates that self-possession is possible. Our imagined therapist of this girl, who is so fortunate in one respect and so unfortunate in another, will already have guessed the paths that therapist and patient might take. Perhaps she will reject the heart physically. She might reject it psychologically, so that she remains always bitter and divided, someone with an enemy at her heart; the effort at self-possession can fail. It would fail just as much if the patient were to deny the problem and live out her guilt in secret and symptomatic ways.

But it is conceivable that a deal might be struck with her realities: if the true pain as well as the good fortune of her circumstances were acknowledged, a richer, more complicated, and knowing person might emerge. It would not be easy or without paradox. Indeed, its emergence might be very like a work of art, this work of heart, as was said of Cézanne: "The main problem was how to relate all of the chaos and disarray of perceptions from nature into a complex but truthful image." At its best the result was "animated by contrasts and unified by analogies." It is not, I think, pretentious to conceive our own work in this light.

CHAPTER 10

THE FUTURE
OF HEALING

The future belongs to psychiatry because finding a safe place for the psyche, the individual life, is its central concern. The concern is biological, neurological, psychological, and sociological: psychiatry is the only systematic study that addresses human life from all these perspectives. This is more than an academic advantage—threats to human existence come from lesions of brain and body, unconscious conflict, and the isolation, domination, and submission found everywhere in social life. The protectors of human existence must confront all these dangers.

Put another way, psychiatry stands four-square between medicine on the one hand, with its technology of recordings, quantitation, and an increasing mastery of bodily ills, and on the other the broad range of psychological, anthropological, and sociological disciplines, extending out to religion and the humanities, healing cults, and all the many groups and institutions devoted to human well-being. Psychiatry gains its immense strength from its capacity to draw on all these forces, to test and retest their contributions, to institutionalize and deinstitutionalize itself along new lines, to organize cohorts of helping professionals as medicine has done, to consider not only sex but sexism. What I wish to discuss in detail is how psychiatry should be viewed just as the medicine of the body is viewed: as an ordinary accompaniment on the journey through life.

This heavy responsibility would hardly be bearable, now or in the past, were it not for the way in which psychiatry's successive tasks have been historically delegated. There is, for example, no way by which the extraordinary growth of demand for psychoanalytically oriented psychotherapy over the last forty years could have been met by analysts and psychiatrists alone. Instead, analysts contributed prominently to the curricula of social-work schools; psychoanalysis became part of psychology; nurse practitioners were supervised and trained by psychiatrists. The present competitive relationship between social work, psychology, and psychiatry is in significant measure a result of psychiatry's own efforts. Above all, it is an answer to a public demand that shows few signs of abating.

The same process is readily illustrated from the biological side. Today we observe the resurgence of that sturdy hybrid, neuropsychiatry. Such was the case at the turn of the century, notably in the work of Carl Wernicke and the early Freud, then around mid-century when lobotomy, convulsive therapy, and insulin-coma therapy appeared. Only a little later lithium's action on aggression and mania was discovered in Australia. The turn of the century was the time of neuropsychiatry's most decisive victories over its diseases. In 1887 Julius Wagner von Jauregg formed the hypothesis that he waited thirty years to test successfully. In 1917, while professor of psychiatry at the University of Vienna and during the breakup of the Austro-Hungarian Empire, Wagner-Jauregg and his assistants took the courageous step of injecting malarial parasites into syphilitic patients. The resulting fevers destroyed the spirochetes in the brains of the tertiary syphilitics and earned him the Nobel Prize. Another thirty years later, the fever treatment of syphilis was succeeded by the use of penicillin, and within two years brain syphilis largely disappeared. Fever treatment, I was told, had been an excellent treatment, but penicillin essentially wiped out tertiary syphilis. Those who watched this event told me they were astonished by it. The patients who had once comprised a fifth of all admissions to mental hospitals simply came no more.

It was also in the early decades of this century that vitamin-deficiency psychoses were first efficiently treated. For many parts of the world this was an event of stunning significance, and, like so many truly successful medical interventions, it has receded from memory. There is something troubling here. Since the first part of the century, and despite extraordinary biological advances of many kinds, we have not seen a single victory of similar magnitude. Not even the lithium treatment of mania can be said to have had a comparable effect. The hiatus in major discoveries suggests that our patients' conditions remain elusive. There is simply no guarantee that future biological advances will have the conclusive effect on mental illness that is hoped for.

Again recall the historical delegation of psychiatry's responsibilities. When a truly successful biological treatment of a psychiatric disorder appears, that disorder often ceases to fall within the province of psychiatrists. This is partly a facet of the necessary specialization of the complex body of medicine. Practicing pharmacologists, internists, and practitioners of those subspecialties of internal medicine that cluster around disorders once considered psychiatric, including not only syphilis and vitamin deficiency but once also tuberculosis and Parkinsonism, take over the care of these disorders. Adequate prescribing requires an elaborate background and experience in physiology and pharmacology. Psychiatrists, that is, physicians, concerned with the remaining disorders, those to whom psychic and social influences still seem the most relevant or at least applicable, often cannot command the skills and knowledge to do both. Of course this may not be the future: the new psychiatrist may well be capable of doing both. Further, the subtlety of chemical interventions may become so great as to require psychological discrimination at the highest level. In that case there would be a true union of chemical and psychological skills.

Surely differences in temperament must also affect the delegation. Popular images of the psychiatrist are very different from those of, say, the surgeon. Such portraits refer to aspects of interest and ability that are fundamental to clinical work: the eagerness to act or listen, control or set free, live with certainty or uncertainty, and above all the capacity to tolerate, even enjoy, different problems. The surgeon cannot shrink from the sight of blood. The psychiatrist must be equally accepting of grief and terror. Granted that much of modern psychiatry springs from such neurologists and neuropathologists as Jean-Martin Charcot, Freud, and Adolf Meyer, and that the chemically trained John Whitehorn contributed, as chief of the Phipps clinic, to the psychological understanding and treatment of psychosis; granted too that many of the neuropsychiatrists coming into positions of academic leadership today will find themselves drawn by their clinical responsibilities toward the psychological and sociological—these shifts of attention and contribution indicate where the life of psychiatry prominently resides.

The enthusiastic neuropsychiatrist will respond, "You are assuming that future knowledge of the brain will not include knowledge and treatment measures for all psychiatric disorders." That is exactly what I am assuming. My reasons follow.

In this century there has occurred a striking growth in the population of psychiatric patients, despite the loss of tertiary syphilitics and vitamin-deficient patients. (I mean by the population of psychiatric patients those who are seen by professional workers in mental health.) Of course this is because of the large rise in the number of practitioners, but there are other reasons as well. We are no longer specialists sequestered behind the walls of forbidding institutions. This momentous change required little more than one generation. Furthermore, people have decided to seek help for what are best called characterological and situational complaints. These are the patients who come and say, "My life isn't going right" or "My life has no meaning," who describe general dissatisfaction, loss of purpose, feelings of going through the motions, and often without any of the traditional psychiatric symptoms or signs. Then there are many others without the traditional complaints but with specific complaints of a different sort. One man hates his job or his boss, one woman can't get married or is afraid to get divorced (a cynic has said that marriage is a great cage with most of those inside trying to get out and most of those on the outside trying to get in).

Some say these are really not psychiatric patients, that they should go, for example, to the clergy. But often they have come from the clergy. Moreover, I can't imagine that psychiatrists want them excluded. This is not because others besides psychiatrists should not treat them, but because psychiatry has always been in the forefront of their investigation and treatment. It is remarkable how much of the fundamental work in this area has been done by physicians: Freud himself, Ludwig Binswanger, Jung, Reich, Sullivan, and in our own time Kernberg and Kohut.

Others say that characterological and situational states are really depression, anxiety, or prepsychotic conditions, to be treated pharmacologically. That is sometimes the case, but seldom exclusively so. The pharmacological treatment of symptoms is unwisely undertaken without detailed consideration of both the patient's character and his or her situation. Otherwise symptom relief may serve to postpone difficult decisions that contribute to the symptoms, or symptom relief may serve the tyrannical purposes of someone by whom the patient is threatened. This is not to say that symptoms should not be relieved or rash decisions postponed. The point is that symptoms, character, and situation should all be considered. Here the official diagnostic scheme misleads us. Because the emphasis is now on the condition inside the patient and not on the adaptation to biological, social, and psychological factors that marked the former system, adaptive difficulties are given relatively short shrift. Adjustment reactions are adjustment disorders, even though the disorder may be outside the patient, not inside, and just as much in need of attention. Of course many situational states are characterological disorders, that is, the patient's modes of reaction are what need attention. Yet in practice, as I have illustrated, it is seldom easy to determine where the principal lesions lie, whether in the body, in the unconscious, in modes of adaptation, in the difficulties of others, in the interaction among them, or in someone's values. Nowhere in psychiatry more than in the treatment of characterological and situational problems is the practitioner more poorly served by sectarian attitudes.

Characterological disorders include the psychopathic states I have already discussed, which has meant a large addition to the ranks of patients. Here again physicians have been in the forefront of investigation and experiment—Gregory Zilboorg, Franz Alexander, Harvey Cleckley, Adelaide Johnson, George Vaillant—names that rank only a little below August Aichhorn's. While the police and the courts have sent us more and more psychopathic patients, and addictions of many kinds, we have recruited our own, in the growing realization of the commonness of "as if" personalities, false personalities, the long list of those living lives other than their own, impostors either by choice or because life has forced on them roles different from those they would have wished.

Here too we must include a group of cases still considered rare, although I believe they are the prototype for a very common disorder. I refer to *folie à deux*. These generally involve young, passive people who have come under the influence of an older, more powerful personality whose paranoid delusions they have learned to share and imitate. Nor is it only delusion for two: I have observed three, four, or five people caught up in such systems. Further, there are those who would argue that the whole German nation was controlled this way by Hitler. It is easy to imagine the existence of less virulent, less complete examples on many levels.

By situational disorders I mean the adjustment reactions now extended from adolescence into every succeeding phase of life, so greatly illuminated, for example, by Erik Erikson and Daniel Levinson: mid-life crises, late-life crises, the very large number of difficult adjustments that need attunement. The contributions of Jean Baker-Miller, Nancy Chodorow, and Carol Gilligan to the developmental psychology of women can prove extremely important here: they may well recast the categories in which discussions of development have gone forward, and have significant effects on the understanding of both sexes. I predict that the time is not far off when medical students and residents, psychology interns, social-work students, nursing students, all the growing numbers of ourselves and our colleagues, will study texts very different from the ones most popular today. These texts will describe the troublesome human situations most common in life, so that students meeting patients will have their clinical imaginations shocked with not only the usual complexes of the unconscious, the biological possibilities, and the diagnostic possibilities, but also the range of situational possibilities. There will be on hand differential diagnoses of the various human situations that may have played a part in precipitating a patient's initial complaint. What is going on in the life of the paranoid married woman of thirty-two or the catatonic boy of seventeen just sent home from college? Such knowledge will be an enormous help because it will allow therapists easier access to the reality of their patients' lives.

Such are some of the characterological and situational problems that crowd more and more of our hospitals and practices. There is another closely related reason why knowledge of brain will not be the principal preserve of future psychiatrists. This has to do with what we have been learning about family life. Today institutions of all kinds are being thrown open to scrutiny— government, schools, above all families—so that transactions once thought private may be observed and broadcast to the world at large. Whatever we think about this, it is happening and, at least in the case of the study and teaching of family therapy, electronic technology has been very helpful indeed. Again, psychiatrists have been in the forefront.

Remember that psychiatry has one great advantage over general medicine: it never divorced itself from public health, as did medicine and surgery. For psychiatrists, the public sources of disease, the public responsibility for the care of disease, have never been foreign. So it is fitting that situational disorders should have a prominent place in its lexicon.

These almost limitless opportunities are the chief source of a continuing crisis, that of delivering care to a quickly growing population of patients from an inadequate base of knowledge, money, and skill. Everyone is familiar with the result. A new clinic opens, and its psychologists, doctors, social workers, and nurses want to study five new patients each day, treat perhaps ten more. But twenty appear the first day, twenty more the second. Someone suggests a list of priorities: acute or emergency cases first and the chronic ones later; or severe disabilities first and then milder ones. Neither system works—too many acute cases prove chronic, demand additional care for husband or mother, and end up occupying half the therapists, or the severe cases do that from the start and depress the staff in addition. The clinic must close its door to new patients after a week of operation, or begin to treat lightly. Drugs are dispensed in great quantities, patients reassured and quickly sent on their way or gathered in large groups like calisthenics classes. Efforts must be made to avoid studying the cases carefully, for fear of uncovering more problems than can be resolved. Gradually the staff leaves for private practice to do what they want at their own pace.

The problem is that the great bulk of patients have chronic psychological disabilities. The acute manifestations were half-treated or neglected altogether, leaving behind unmourned losses, conflicts still active after many years, fundamental sore points long put out of mind. Therapists coming on the scene can deal only with the superficial problems and then are blamed for not achieving larger or more permanent change. The mental-health movement, revived every thirty or forty years, founders on this one fact: chronicity. A psychotic episode lasts a few weeks or months; confusion, hallucinations, and bizarre gestures all disappear, but the person who recovers may seem less alive than he did when psychotic. Once this was true of physical illness. In seventeenth-century England, it was nothing to harbor open boils, rashes, rheumatisms, as well as deep-running infections and cancers. Families of ten lost five or six by early death. The population of one English city was halved three times in a single century. Charles MacLaurin gives an account of the deaths and diseases of royalty that reads like terminal reports of an alcoholic ward in Bellevue. Kings who received what medicines there were died from half a dozen diseases, if they did not die from the medicines. Life ended in a few decades, and many were half-dead years before they died. You can go to any poor country in Asia today and see the same physical wreckage.

How then can I claim that an understaffed, underfinanced, disputatious, often ignorant psychiatric profession, at one moment fanatically certain and the next almost hopelessly uncertain, owns the future? Such a claim would seem to illustrate what critics of psychiatry often assert, that it is a profession most notable for unwarranted declarations and exaggerated hopes.

In reply, I suggest that psychiatry's hold on the future will be a result of several changes, each already beginning to show itself. First, psychiatry will follow medicine's program of specialization, and as part of that program increasingly recruit other health professionals to carry out the varied parts of mental-health care. Today only a small portion of the actual care of patients is done by physicians and surgeons. Most of the work is undertaken by nurses, nurse practitioners, nursing assistants, physiotherapists, or pharmacists—the list is long and constantly growing. As our knowledge of psychotherapy increases, natural subdivisions of the work will emerge. For example, supportive psychotherapy, so long disdained, yet perhaps the most complex of all psychological interventions, will call forth subspecialties that far transcend in power and subtlety such current activities as skill training and remoralization.

Furthermore, our relationship to the popular conceptions of health and disease will change. Not long ago, physical disease, for all its commonness and chronicity, and perhaps because of its mystery, aroused terror and shame. To be sick was to be possessed, defective. Illness did not excuse a man; it marked him. I suspect that the same change is already occurring in relation to psychiatric conditions. With it should come a change in the relationship to therapists: a greater and earlier eagerness to consult. We can already see some change in the lessening of the severity and bizarreness of symptoms (note how little dramatic chronic catatonia is seen), which, I suspect, is a function of the relatively greater ease and speed of referral possible today.

Few now expect perfect physical health, never to break a leg, catch a cold, or have one's appendix out. A long series of predictable physical illnesses awaits us at every age, laid down in statistics and almost as certain as death. Just as many psychological troubles await us, but not so many take them for granted. Most people still expect not to get emotionally sick or face fresh crises with each stage of life.

Yet listen to everyday talk. It is commonplace to hear people called paranoid, even schizoid; unconscious impulses are acknowledged and, perhaps most important, the mystery of human nature is increasingly appreciated. The largest part of a man, to cite Emerson again, is that which is not inventoried. We are all now and then guilty of the folly of judging others at a glance, across a crowded room. It is the nature of first opinions to classify: in or out, strong or weak, dumb or smart, shrewd or naive, each group of scholars or politicians using its own needs to classify the race. At root the judgments are tribal: does the observed belong, or can I defeat him? This is not folly at the city gates in a time of siege. But it is if we mean to understand human nature and not be admissions officers to our little aristocracies.

Soon it will be usual to weigh people psychologically—to determine how much they have locked up in the past, how much free energy they have for the present and future, the state of their relationships and personal capacities. We will have psychological aptitude tests that have nothing to do with determinations of manual skills or lines of work. The wise man wants to know not only what he can do but the skills he has for life and the further preparation he needs. It is common for a man to say he plays golf poorly or can't run fast, even that he has a weak head for figures; we learn these limitations in school and business. But how many recognize their personal limitations, of vastly more importance? Individuals, generous in other preparations, enter relationships that last decades, bear children, shape a neighborhood as if they were climbing a mountain barefoot— and are surprised, helpless, and angry at the poor results.

The contrast with our attitudes toward physical disabilities is startling. It is nothing for a man to be checked over annually. But who keeps track of his interests, relationships, skills at changing jobs, his replacement of lost friends? Indeed, the burgeoning array of physical concerns crowds out psychological ones: forty years ago a physician might note how anxious a patient was, or even ask, but now the availability of twenty blood tests leaves time for nothing else. Is it a function of our commercial culture or the present level of human development that we use tests of vocational ability and physical capacity and largely neglect other human functions? I know people who can coordinate their finger movements at a great rate and don't understand their children after thirty years of parenthood.

Psychiatry will also follow medicine in its acceptance of whatever pathogenetic processes and agents are discovered. So far, sectarianism has dominated such acceptance. Biological psychiatry is willing to accept viral, toxic, enzymatic, or chromosomal agents of psychiatric disorders. Yet it shows a strange reluctance to acknowledge the pathogenetic properties of that large human organism of which we are all examples. When one considers the evolutionary path we are said to have followed, with its predatory victories and extraordinary examples of induced submissiveness, it would be surprising if the same patterns of domination and submission were not a social commonplace. It is true that in some parts of the world the old forms of predation and submission, cannibalism and slavery, have disappeared. Yet it is equally true that these physical manifestations of master and slave have often been replaced by psychological forms, and that at least some psychopathological findings are the result of psychological domination and submission. I make these statements not in a spirit of partisan reluctance to admit genetic and unconscious pathological processes. Quite the opposite: I am expecting an eagerness to acknowledge, along with general medicine, a great many phenomena as the sources of our patients' problems.

This recognition of our evolutionary heritage leads to the final reason for psychiatry's claim on the future. It is reported that Gandhi, asked what he thought of Western civilization, responded, ''That would be a good idea.'' Faced with intermittent warfare, national and religious rivalries, the threat of nuclear annihilation, the observer of contemporary life must assent. I have suggested that what we mean by civilization is largely our replacement of cannibalism and physical enslavement by their psychological equivalents. That is to say, genuine human respect, giving others their freedom, the capacity to protect one's own freedom and self, all these are rare. Predation and slavery continue among us in the sense of psychological invasiveness and compliance. I believe that psychiatry has a great role to play in defining the conditions of human self-respect and freedom, as well as in helping individuals achieve this in their own lives.

I am not proposing a new community-health movement with even more grandiose goals, nor am I proposing a direction for psychiatry that will remove it further from medicine. What I am proposing is very medical indeed.

Psychiatry is still largely without workable tests for normality, a deficiency that separates it sharply from medical practice. We all know how central to medicine are the taking of pulse and respiratory rates, the testing of reflexes, and a hundred other readily determined tests of health. In psychiatry we have few such measures, and for this reason the findings of a psychiatrist have an ominous ring. These findings are not seen, as medical findings are, in the context of the whole human body and situation. So psychiatrists use single adjectives to describe their patients, calling them manic, neurotic, or schizophrenic, as if they were all this or that, as I have done. Such a practice is rare in medicine, where the patient is not tuberculous or cancerous but has a local lesion of a specific organ.

I predict that as we learn to define "human being" and to determine the extent to which it is present, then psychiatrists, like general medical practitioners, will stop talking adjectivally and begin to see the patients' conditions in perspective. I also predict that this effort will be tied into the problem of freedom and self-respect just mentioned. That is, psychiatrists, having their central interest in the individual self, will play a strong role in the nurturance of this peculiarly human aspect of evolutionary development. The psyche, as much as the body, needs a safe place in which to recover or be healed.

Let me recall where I began, with one doctor talking to another, in a kind of shadowed mutuality, a doctor who was also a patient. Now, at the end, I am talking to doctors and patients and people at large, hoping that a safe place can be made between us in which this great work will be done—to give dignity to the commonplace, to let sad and frightened voices speak, to sing "close to the music of what happens," to set free.

NOTES

1. MY DOCTOR

Sigmund Freud's principal descriptions of psychoanalytic technique are presented in volume 12 of *The Standard Edition of the Complete Psychological Works*; see especially "Recommendations to Physicians Practicing Psychoanalysis."

Donald Winnicott has influenced the whole presentation of this book. Of particular relevance to my thinking is his *The Maturational Processes and the Facilitating Environment* (New York: International Universities Press, 1965); for "letting alone," see especially pp. 29–36. I could as well have referred to my old teacher, Elvin Semrad, on which this book is so dependent. See that fine collection of his sayings, *Semrad: The Heart of a Therapist*, ed. Susan Rako and Harvey Mazer (New York: Aronson, 1980), for example: "The most mature people, wherever they find themselves, are comfortable enough with themselves that they can live alone in the presence of other people. It's paradoxical, but mature object relationships are essentially relations where two or more people can live alone with each other" (p. 48).

2. FREUD'S INVENTION

Richard Wilbur, "The Writer," reprinted in *New and Collected Poems* (San Diego: Harcourt Brace Jovanovich, 1988), p. 72.

The element of contradiction in creative thought has been demonstrated by Albert Rothenberg in *The Emerging Goddess* (Chicago: University of Chicago Press, 1979).

For the claims made here, and in Chapter 10, about physical health in earlier times, see Charles MacLaurin, *Mere Mortals* (New York: Doran, 1925).

3. WORDS AS DEEDS

J. L. Austin, *How To Do Things with Words* (Cambridge: Harvard University Press, 1962, 1975).

Joseph Conrad, *Chance: A Tale in Two Parts* (New York: Doubleday, Page, 1924), p. 212. I am indebted to Jack Green for calling my attention to this passage.

Primo Levi, *Survival in Auschwitz and The Reawakening* (New York: Summit Books, 1986). Faye Mittleman pointed this out.

4. TALKING TO A STRANGER

My discussion of interviewing in this chapter and the next owes much to William James's classic *Principles of Psychology* (1890), especially the chapter on stream of consciousness.

The term "working beside" is elaborated in my *Participant Observation* (New York: Aronson, 1976). For more on "bestride," see my *Making Contact* (Cambridge: Harvard University Press, 1986).

5. RELIABLE FINDINGS

For fuller description of the various psychiatric schools, see my *Approaches to the Mind* (Boston: Little, Brown, 1973; reprint Cambridge: Harvard University Press, 1987).

The work of the two best-known names in current American psychoanalysis, Otto Kernberg and Heinz Kohut, needs to be savored at length. I suggest Kernberg's *Borderline Conditions and Pathological Narcissism* (New York:

Aronson, 1985) and Kohut's *The Restoration of the Self* (New York: International Universities Press, 1977).

For Harry Stack Sullivan's discussion of "the illusion of personal individuality," see his article of that title in *Psychiatry* 13 (1950), 317–332; reprinted in *The Fusion of Psychiatry and Social Science* (New York: W. W. Norton, 1964).

I take up the problem of precision versus reliability in detail elsewhere, in my "The Risks of Knowing and Not Knowing," *Journal of Social and Biological Structure* 5 (1982), 213–222.

6. ANATOMY OF A SUICIDE

René Dubos, *Mirage of Health* (London: Allen and Unwin, 1960), p. 112.

A good introduction to the work of Harry Harlow is "The Heterosexual Affectional System in Monkeys," *American Psychologist* 17 (1962), 1–9.

7. SCHIZOPHRENIA

For an excellent review of the evidence for heterogeneous outcomes (including recoveries) in schizophrenic psychoses, see Courtenay M. Harding, Joseph Zubin, and John S. Strauss, "Chronicity in Schizophrenia: Fact, Partial Fact, or Artifact?" *Hospital and Community Psychiatry* 38 (1987), 477–486.

Freud's statement about the origin of the ego appears in *Group Psychology and the Analysis of the Ego*, volume 18, p. 110, of *The Standard Edition of the Complete Psychological Works*.

The passage from Charles Darwin is found in the conclusion, chapter 15, to *The Origin of Species* (Modern Library edition, p. 371).

8. PSYCHOPATHY

August Aichhorn's major work is *Wayward Youth* (New York: Viking, 1935); the German edition was published in 1925. An important contribution relating this work, Freud's ego ideal, and modern ideas about narcissism is J. M. Murray, "Narcissism and the Ego Ideal," *Journal of the American Psychoanalytic Association* 12 (1964), 477–510.

9. SULLIVAN AND THE HEART

Our understanding of the biological process of world-making owes much to Jakob Baron von Uexküll, *Theoretical Biology* (New York: Harcourt, Brace, 1926).

Sullivan's statement about the ambition-ridden is taken from his *Conceptions of Modern Psychiatry* (New York: W. W. Norton, 1953), pp. 208–209.

The claim that schizophrenia may not be identifiable is made by Harrison Pope, Jr., Bruce M. Cohen, and Joseph F. Lipinski from the Mailman Research Center, McLean Hospital, Belmont, Massachusetts, in an unpublished article, "Is Schizophrenia a Meaningful Diagnosis?" (personal communication).

Here are two examples of what I call the European hierarchical system of thinking, from Erik Erikson, "Elements of a Psychoanalytic Theory of Psychosocial Development," in *The Course of Life*, vol. 1: *Infancy and Early Childhood*, ed. S. I. Greenspan and G. H. Pollack (New York: NIMH, 1980):

"As I now quote what the embryologist has to tell us about the epigenesis of organ systems, I hope the reader will 'hear' the probability that growth and development follows analogous patterns." (p. 18)
"To us, it is first of all important to realize that in the sequence of significant experiences, the healthy child, if properly guided, can be trusted to conform to the epigenetic laws of development as they now create a succession of potentialities for significant interaction with a growing number of individuals and with the mores that govern them." (p. 19)

The best introduction to Lawrence Kohlberg's work is *The Psychology of Moral Development* (New York: Harper 1985).

The comments on Cézanne are by Nicholas Wadley, *Cézanne and His Art* (New York: Galahad Books, 1975).

10. THE FUTURE OF HEALING

Singing "close to the music of what happens" is Seamus Heaney's wonderful image from his poem "Song" in *Field Work* (New York: Farrar, Straus and Giroux, 1979), p. 56.

Earlier versions of some of these chapters have appeared in *Contemporary Psychoanalysis* (Chapter 5), *New England Journal of Medicine* (Chapter 6), *Journal of the American Medical Association* (Chapter 7), and *Psychotherapy and Psychosomatics* (Chapter 10). I thank the publishers for permission to reuse this material.

INDEX